Be a cool calculator this summer with CGP!

Thirsty for summer Maths practice? This Daily Practice Book from CGP
is more refreshing than an orange ice-lolly during a heatwave...

Inside, you'll find a page of Maths practice for every school day of the
summer term, covering a huge range of skills from the Year 4 curriculum.

It's perfect for use in class or at home, with plenty of examples
and some colourful fun to make sure pupils stay chilled!

What CGP is all about

Our sole aim here at CGP is to produce the highest quality books
— carefully written, immaculately presented and
dangerously close to being funny.

Then we work our socks off to get them out to you
— at the cheapest possible prices.

Contents

Published by CGP

ISBN: 978 1 78908 654 6

Editors: Katie Fernandez, Sarah Pattison, Rachael Rogers, George Wright
With thanks to Glenn Rogers and Emma Wright for the proofreading.
With thanks to Lottie Edwards for the copyright research.

Clipart from Corel®

Printed by Zenith Print and Packaging Ltd, Pontypridd.
Based on the classic CGP style created by Richard Parsons.

How to Use this Book

- This book contains 60 daily practice tests.

- We've split them into 12 sections — that's roughly one for each week of the Year 4 summer term.

- Each week is made up of 5 tests, so there's one for every school day of the term (Monday – Friday).

- Each test should take about 10 minutes to complete.

- The tests contain a mix of topics from Year 4 Maths. New Year 4 topics are gradually introduced as you go through the book.

- The tests increase in difficulty as you progress through the term.

- The last three weeks recap topics from throughout Year 4 Maths.

- Each test looks something like this:

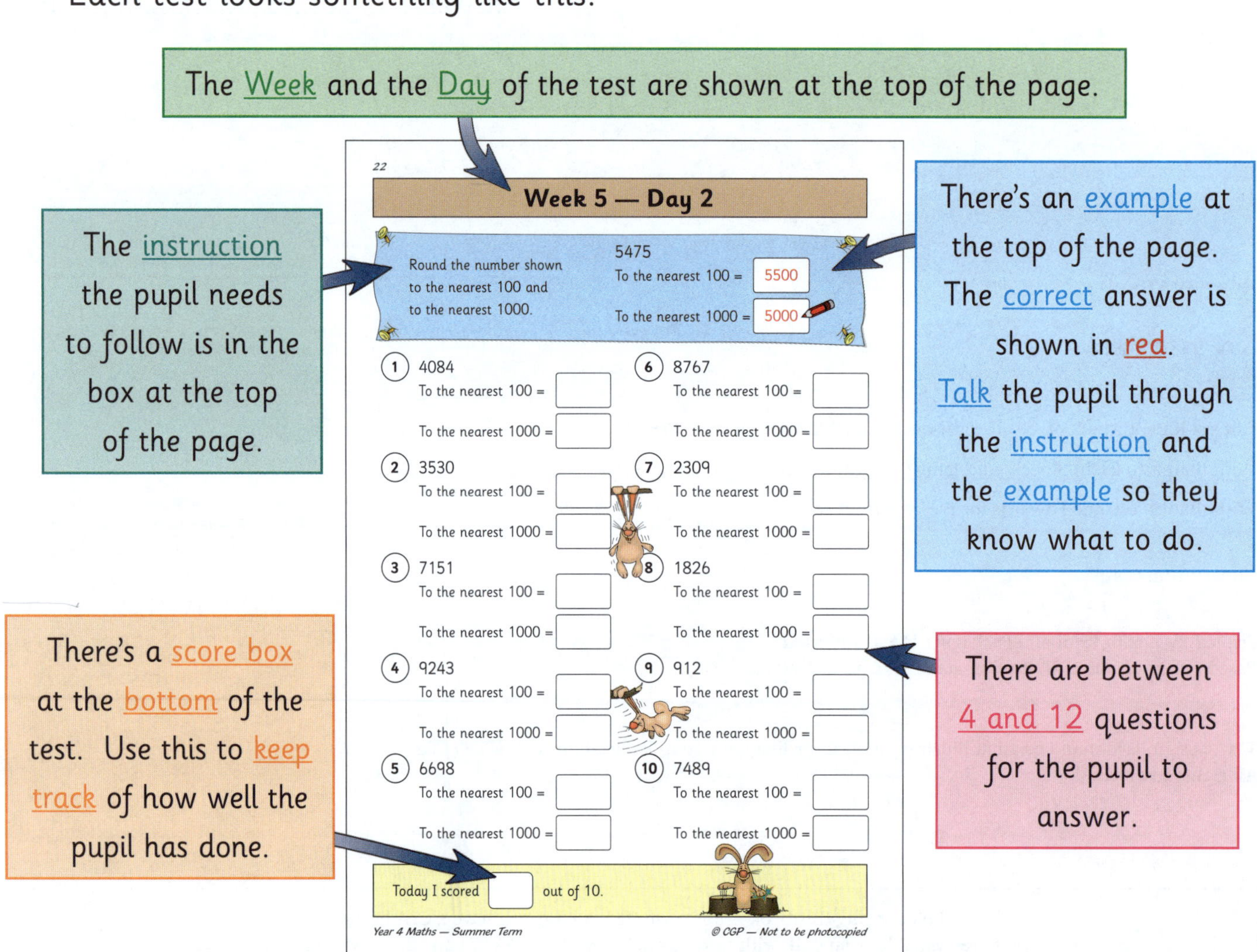

Week 1 — Day 1

Write the next three numbers in the sequence.

| 0 | , | 25 | , | 50 | , | 75 | , | 100 | , | 125 |

1) 300 , 400 , 500 , ___ , ___ , ___

2) 600 , 650 , 700 , ___ , ___ , ___

3) 1000 , 2000 , 3000 , ___ , ___ , ___

4) 350 , 375 , 400 , ___ , ___ , ___

5) 6600 , 7600 , 8600 , ___ , ___ , ___

6) 875 , 900 , 925 , ___ , ___ , ___

7) 7015 , 6015 , 5015 , ___ , ___ , ___

8) 1250 , 1225 , 1200 , ___ , ___ , ___

Today I scored [ ] out of 8.

Year 4 Maths — Summer Term

Week 1 — Day 2

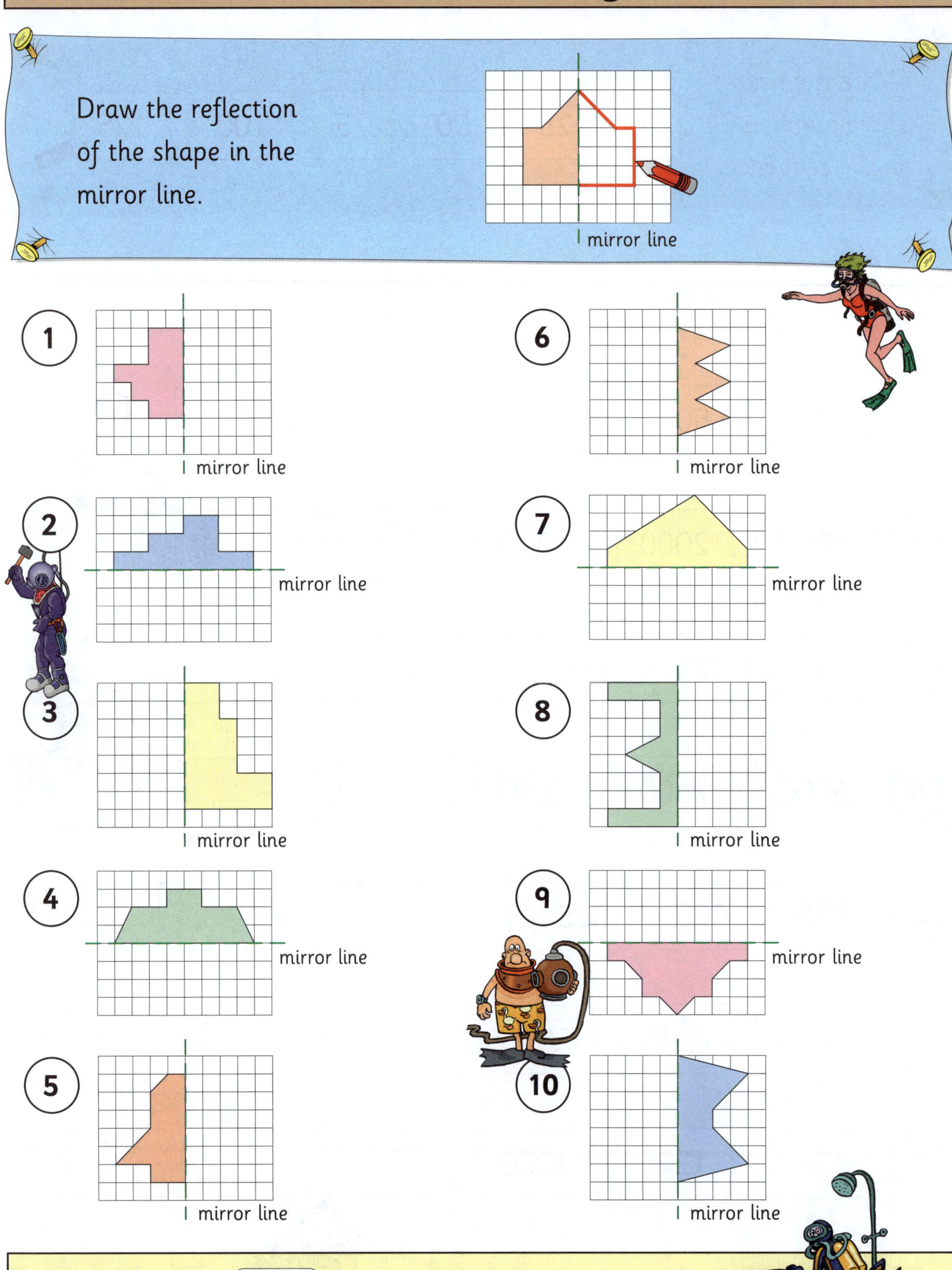

Today I scored [ ] out of 10.

Week 1 — Day 3

Tick the box next to the measurement that is larger.

3300 m ✓

3 km

1 6000 m

6.4 km

2 9500 g

9 kg

3 9900 m

10 km

4 5000 ml

4.7 litres

5 1900 cm

1.9 m

6 700 cm

70 m

7 105 seconds

2 minutes

8 4000 g

400 kg

9 3850 ml

38.5 litres

10 450 minutes

7 hours

11 24 m

2500 mm

12 600 seconds

9.5 minutes

Today I scored ☐ out of 12.

Year 4 Maths — Summer Term

Week 1 — Day 4

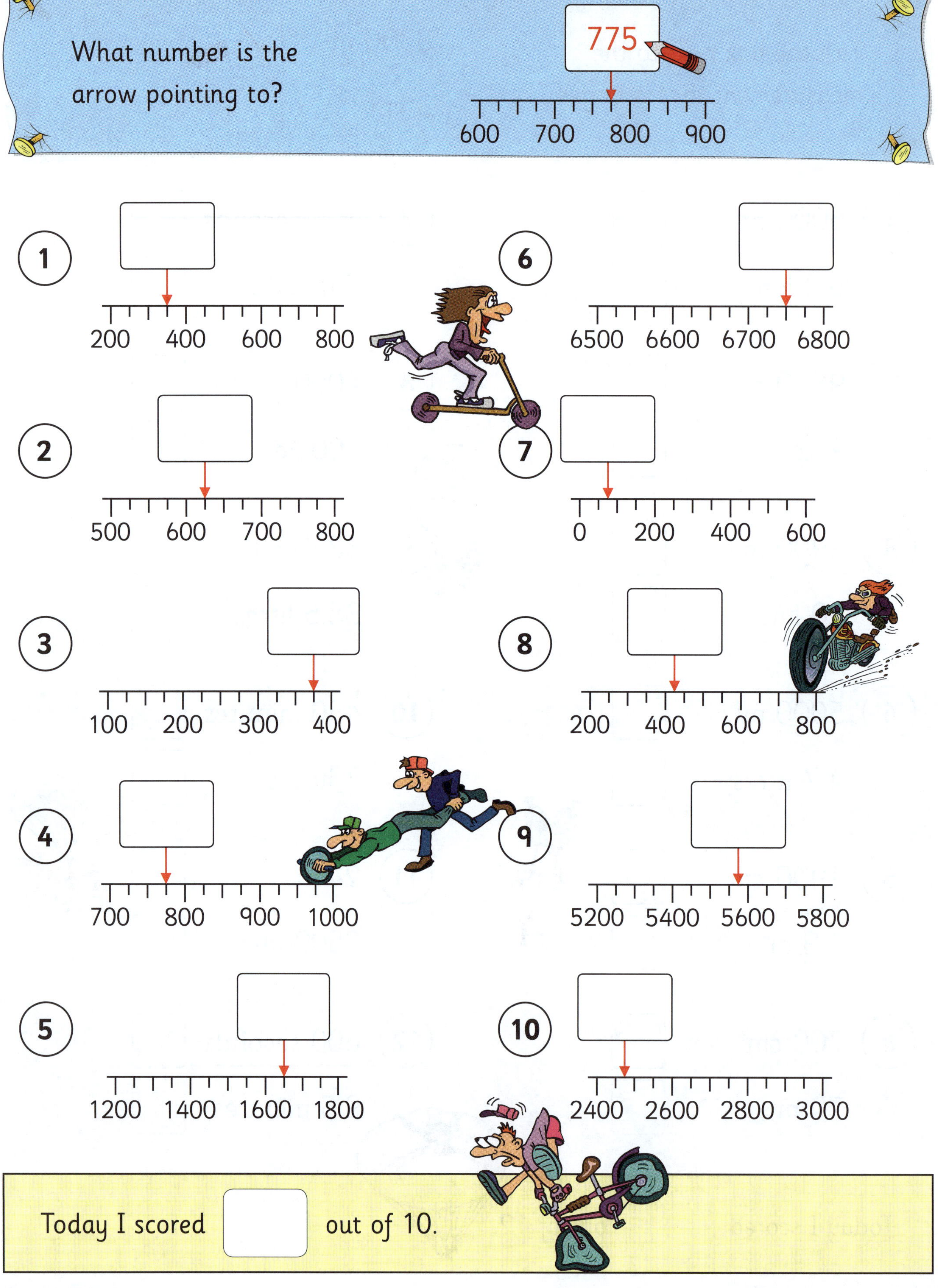

What number is the arrow pointing to?

Today I scored ☐ out of 10.

Week 1 — Day 5

Solve the word problem.

Jim walks 6000 m on Monday.
He walks 1000 m each day afterwards.
How far does he walk in total from
Monday to Thursday?

1 Ralph swims 2000 m on Monday. He swims 1000 m each day afterwards. How far does he swim in total from Monday to Wednesday?

m

2 Abby runs 50 km in January. She runs 25 km each month afterwards. How far does she run in total from January to May?

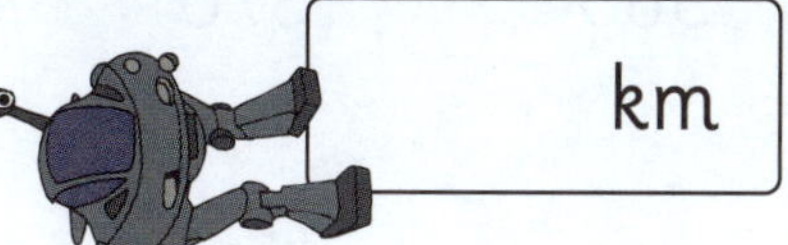

km

3 Carol rows 4000 m on Thursday. She rows 1000 m each day afterwards. How far does she row in total from Thursday to Sunday?

m

4 Elise drives 75 km on Tuesday. She drives 25 km each day afterwards. How far does she drive in total from Tuesday to Sunday?

km

5 Jenny walks 8000 m on Monday. She walks 1000 m each day afterwards. How far does she walk in total from Monday to Friday?

m

6 Aaman kayaks 125 km in July. He kayaks 25 km each month afterwards. How far does he kayak in total from July to January?

km

7 Robin cycles 12 000 m on Sunday. He cycles 1000 m each day afterwards. How far does he cycle in total from Sunday to Saturday?

m

Today I scored ☐ out of 7.

Week 2 — Day 1

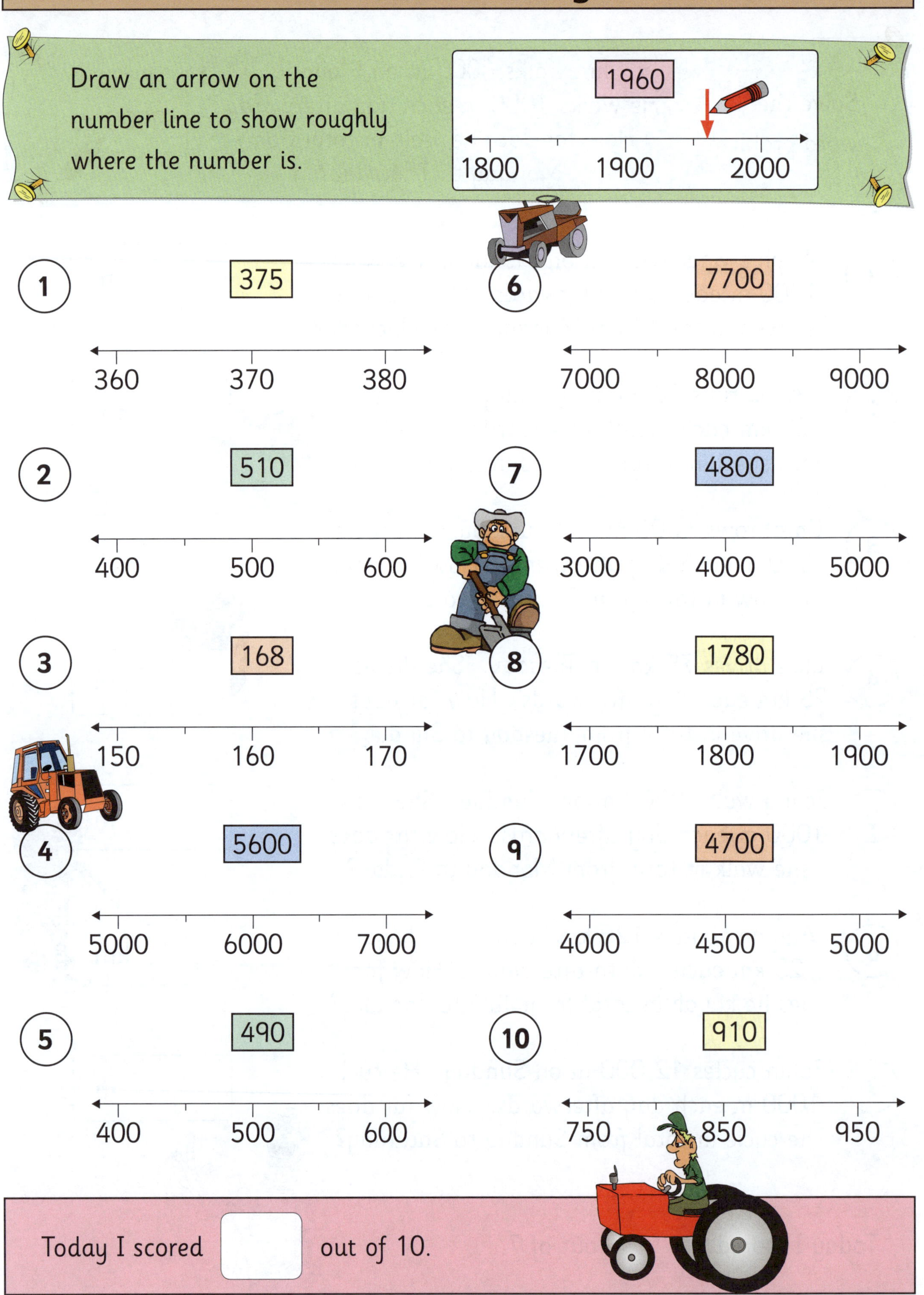

Today I scored ☐ out of 10.

Week 2 — Day 2

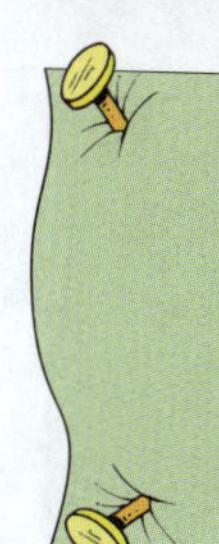

Fill in the box using <, > or =.

$25 + 14 + 9 \boxed{>} 65 - 18$

1) $95 - 43 \;\square\; 31 + 15 + 2$

6) $8 \times 9 \;\square\; 210 \div 3$

2) $23 + 5 + 22 \;\square\; 6 \times 8$

7) $72 \div 12 \;\square\; 43 - 37$

3) $9 \times 6 \;\square\; 77 - 21$

8) $450 \div 9 \;\square\; 91 - 42$

4) $47 + 16 + 4 \;\square\; 640 \div 8$

9) $9 \times 12 \;\square\; 152 - 46$

5) $7 \times 7 \;\square\; 29 + 13 + 8$

10) $9 + 89 + 34 \;\square\; 12 \times 11$

Today I scored $\square$ out of 10.

Year 4 Maths — Summer Term

Week 2 — Day 3

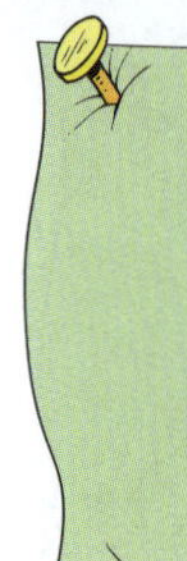

Solve the calculation.

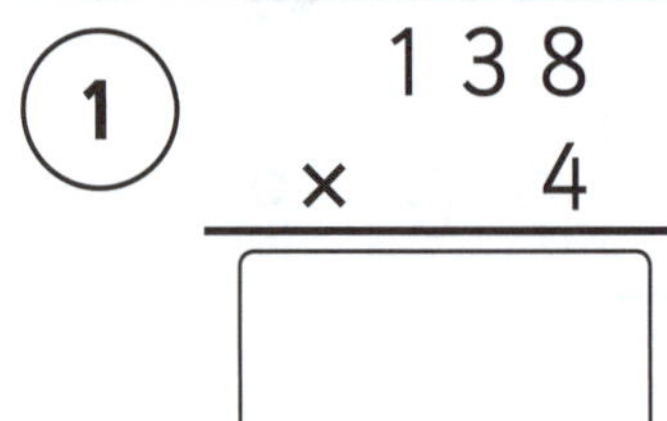

1
$$138 \times 4$$

2
$$164 \times 5$$

3
$$412 \times 3$$

4
$$814 \times 6$$

5
$$435 \times 6$$

6
$$302 \times 8$$

7
$$815 \times 8$$

8
$$426 \times 9$$

9
$$593 \times 7$$

10
$$638 \times 7$$

Today I scored ☐ out of 10.

Week 2 — Day 4

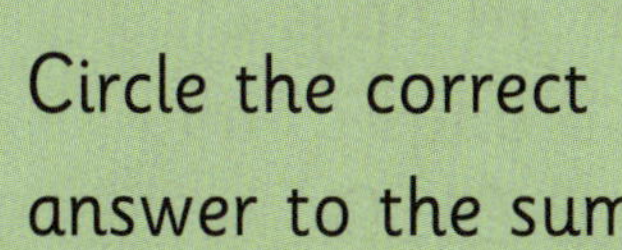

Circle the correct answer to the sum.

XC + LV =

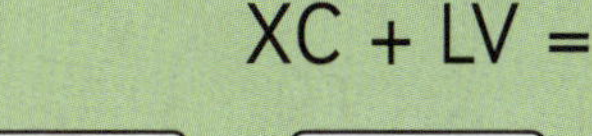

(145)   165   190

1   XXI + XVI =

35   37   42

2   XIV + L =

59   64   66

3   LXI + XXXV =

76   94   96

4   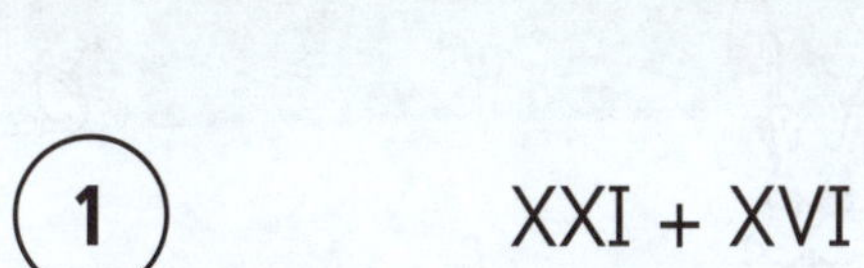C + XLIX =

149   151   159

5   LV + XL = 

95   105   115

6   LXX + XLV =

115   135   155

7   XXVI + XC =

106   116   126

8   LIX + LVI =

115   117   129

9   LXXXV + XCV =

150   180   200

10   XCI + LXV =

156   161   176

Today I scored [ ] out of 10.

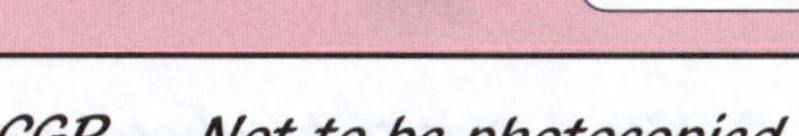

   Year 4 Maths — Summer Term

Week 2 — Day 5

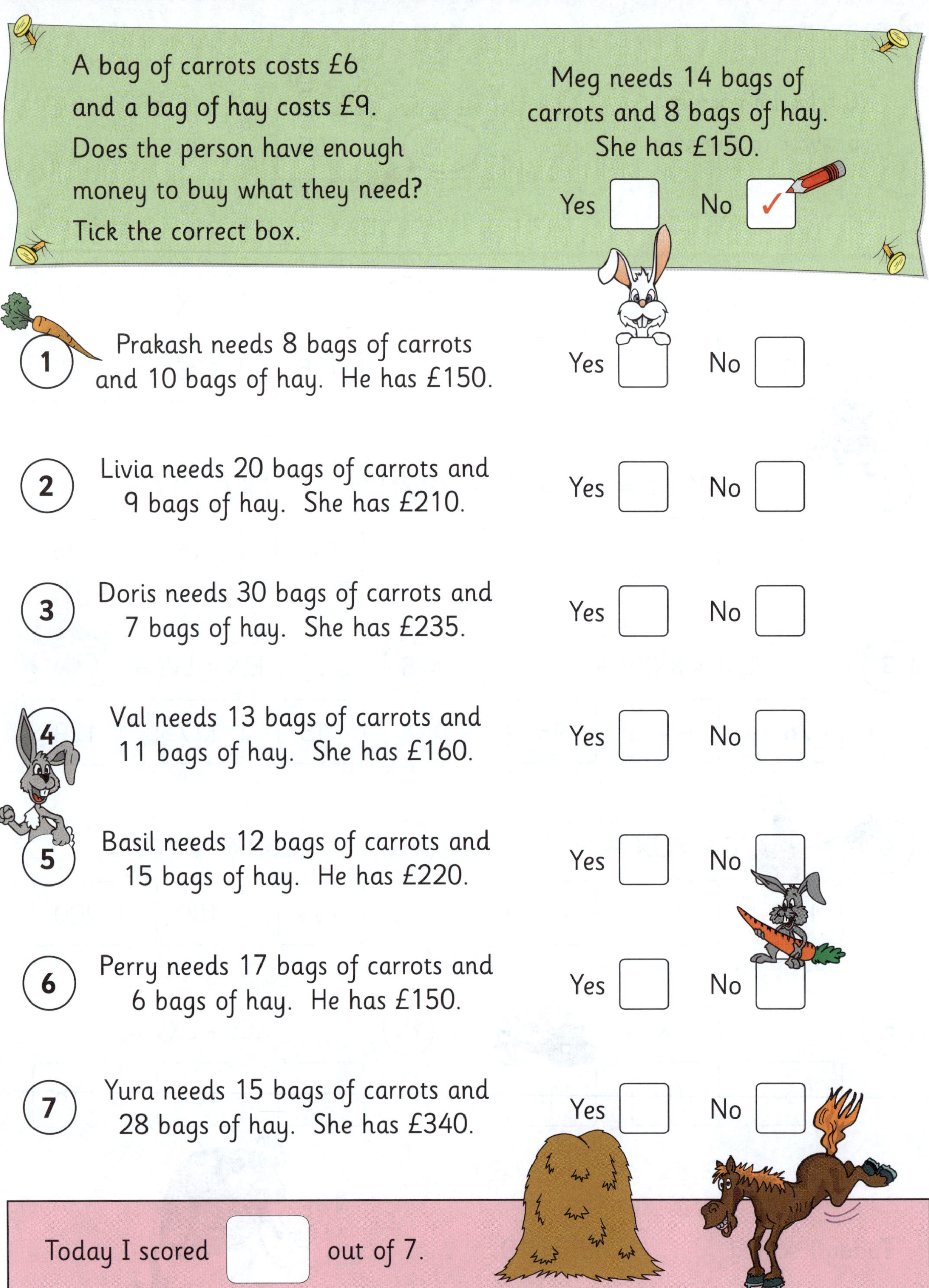

A bag of carrots costs £6 and a bag of hay costs £9. Does the person have enough money to buy what they need? Tick the correct box.

Meg needs 14 bags of carrots and 8 bags of hay. She has £150.

Yes ☐ No ✓

1. Prakash needs 8 bags of carrots and 10 bags of hay. He has £150. Yes ☐ No ☐

2. Livia needs 20 bags of carrots and 9 bags of hay. She has £210. Yes ☐ No ☐

3. Doris needs 30 bags of carrots and 7 bags of hay. She has £235. Yes ☐ No ☐

4. Val needs 13 bags of carrots and 11 bags of hay. She has £160. Yes ☐ No ☐

5. Basil needs 12 bags of carrots and 15 bags of hay. He has £220. Yes ☐ No ☐

6. Perry needs 17 bags of carrots and 6 bags of hay. He has £150. Yes ☐ No ☐

7. Yura needs 15 bags of carrots and 28 bags of hay. She has £340. Yes ☐ No ☐

Today I scored ☐ out of 7.

Week 3 — Day 1

Write two different calculations you could use to work out how many aliens are on the planet. Use one of your calculations to work out the answer.

Planet Zog has 56 aliens. 8 aliens leave, but another 13 arrive.

| $56 - 8 + 13$ | or | $56 + 13 - 8$ |

Answer = 61

1) Planet Mezz has 97 aliens. 8 aliens leave, but another 5 arrive.

[ ] or [ ]   Answer = [ ]

2) Planet Ping has 50 aliens. 19 aliens arrive, but 17 leave.

[ ] or [ ]   Answer = [ ]

3) Planet Tro has 45 aliens. 31 aliens arrive, but 13 leave.

[ ] or [ ]   Answer = [ ]

4) Planet Fi has 14 aliens. 79 aliens arrive, but 22 leave.

[ ] or [ ]   Answer = [ ]

5) Planet Zinger-ding has 72 aliens. 38 aliens leave, but another 57 arrive.

[ ] or [ ]   Answer = [ ]

6) Planet Boggi has 66 aliens. 55 aliens arrive, but 34 leave.

[ ] or [ ]   Answer = [ ]

Today I scored [ ] out of 6.

Year 4 Maths — Summer Term

Week 3 — Day 2

Draw lines between the numbers on each row to show the factor pairs. You won't need to use all of the numbers and not all factor pairs may be possible.

Factor pairs of 20.

| 3 | 5 | 6 | 12 | 2 | 20 |

| 4 | 15 | 40 | 10 | 8 | 1 |

1 Factor pairs of 15.

| 3 | 10 | 7 | 15 | 30 | 14 |

| 0 | 2 | 5 | 6 | 1 | 8 |

5 Factor pairs of 36.

| 4 | 3 | 6 | 1 | 14 | 24 |

| 12 | 8 | 9 | 11 | 36 | 2 |

2 Factor pairs of 21.

| 11 | 1 | 8 | 42 | 7 | 6 |

| 21 | 12 | 20 | 4 | 3 | 2 |

6 Factor pairs of 48.

| 7 | 8 | 2 | 4 | 3 | 48 |

| 9 | 24 | 6 | 40 | 1 | 12 |

3 Factor pairs of 12.

| 2 | 8 | 11 | 12 | 7 | 3 |

| 24 | 6 | 1 | 9 | 4 | 10 |

7 Factor pairs of 100.

| 40 | 25 | 1 | 20 | 15 | 50 |

| 10 | 6 | 5 | 4 | 2 | 75 |

4 Factor pairs of 18.

| 8 | 6 | 7 | 9 | 12 | 1 |

| 4 | 3 | 10 | 18 | 5 | 2 |

8 Factor pairs of 60.

| 10 | 60 | 3 | 4 | 12 | 2 |

| 50 | 6 | 20 | 5 | 30 | 40 |

Today I scored [ ] out of 8.

Week 3 — Day 3

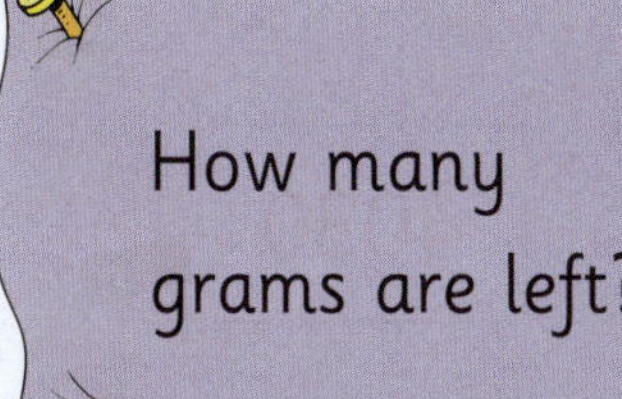

How many grams are left?

A pizza weighs 770 g. Finn eats $\frac{1}{11}$ of the pizza and Joe eats $\frac{2}{7}$.

480 g

1
A portion of apple crumble weighs 180 g.
Chester eats $\frac{1}{9}$ of the portion and Mason eats $\frac{1}{6}$.

g

2
A bar of chocolate weighs 200 g.
Femi eats $\frac{1}{10}$ of the chocolate and Mia eats $\frac{3}{5}$.

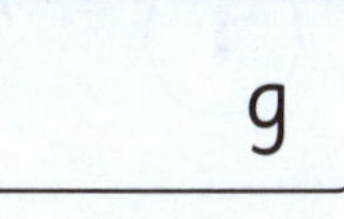

g

3
A lemon tart weighs 240 g.
Lucas eats $\frac{3}{12}$ of the tart and Clayton eats $\frac{1}{3}$.

g

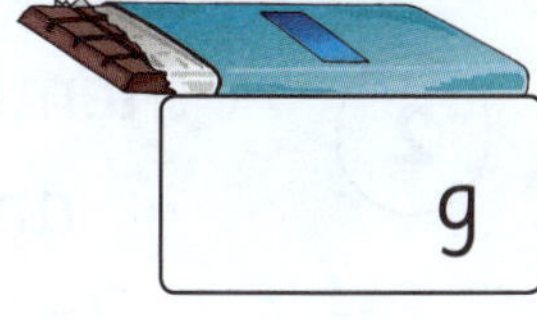

4
A slice of flapjack weighs 90 g.
Vishal eats $\frac{2}{3}$ of the slice and Gita eats $\frac{2}{9}$.

g

5
A pie weighs 600 g.
Luna eats $\frac{3}{6}$ of the pie and Morgan eats $\frac{2}{8}$.

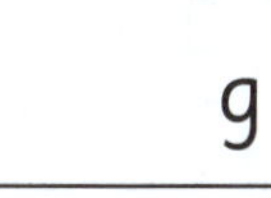

g

6
A cake weighs 360 g.
Josie eats $\frac{4}{9}$ of the cake and Maneet eats $\frac{4}{12}$.

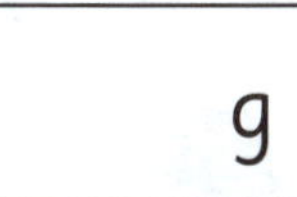

g

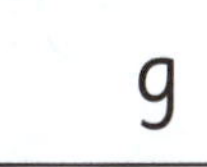

Today I scored [ ] out of 6.

Year 4 Maths — Summer Term

Week 3 — Day 4

How many visitors were not children?

A zoo had 4324 visitors on Friday and 3218 visitors on Saturday. 3512 of the visitors were children.

4030

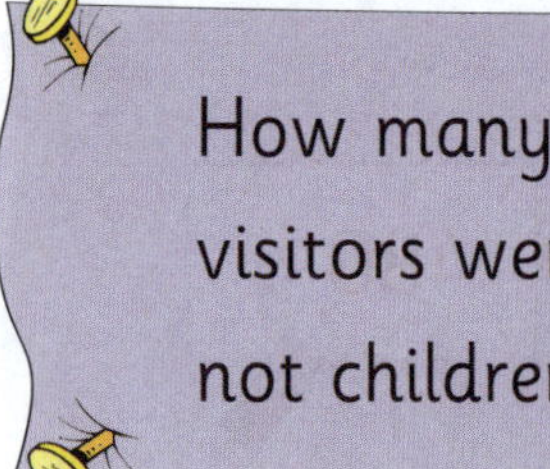

1 A theatre had 1324 visitors on Friday and 1365 visitors on Saturday. 1457 of the visitors were children.

2 A theme park had 2617 visitors on Friday and 4334 visitors on Saturday. 3861 of the visitors were children.

3 A museum had 3516 visitors on Friday and 4755 visitors on Saturday. 2238 of the visitors were children.

4 An ice-rink had 5592 visitors on Friday and 3645 visitors on Saturday. 3546 of the visitors were children.

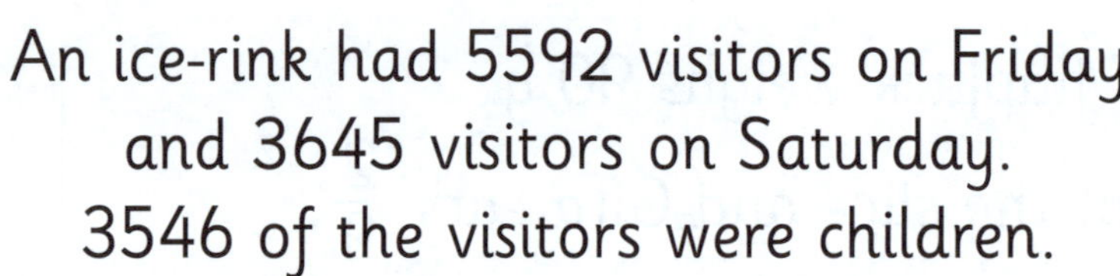

5 A cinema had 1295 visitors on Friday and 2216 visitors on Saturday. 1527 of the visitors were children.

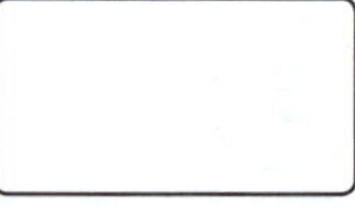

6 A restaurant had 2957 visitors on Friday and 2968 visitors on Saturday. 1926 of the visitors were children.

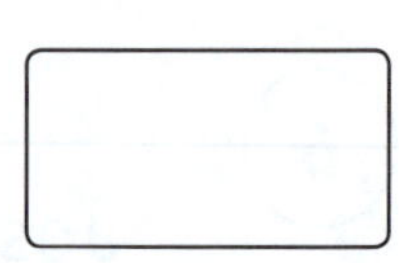

Today I scored ___ out of 6.

Week 3 — Day 5

Complete the diagram so that it shows a pair of equivalent fractions.

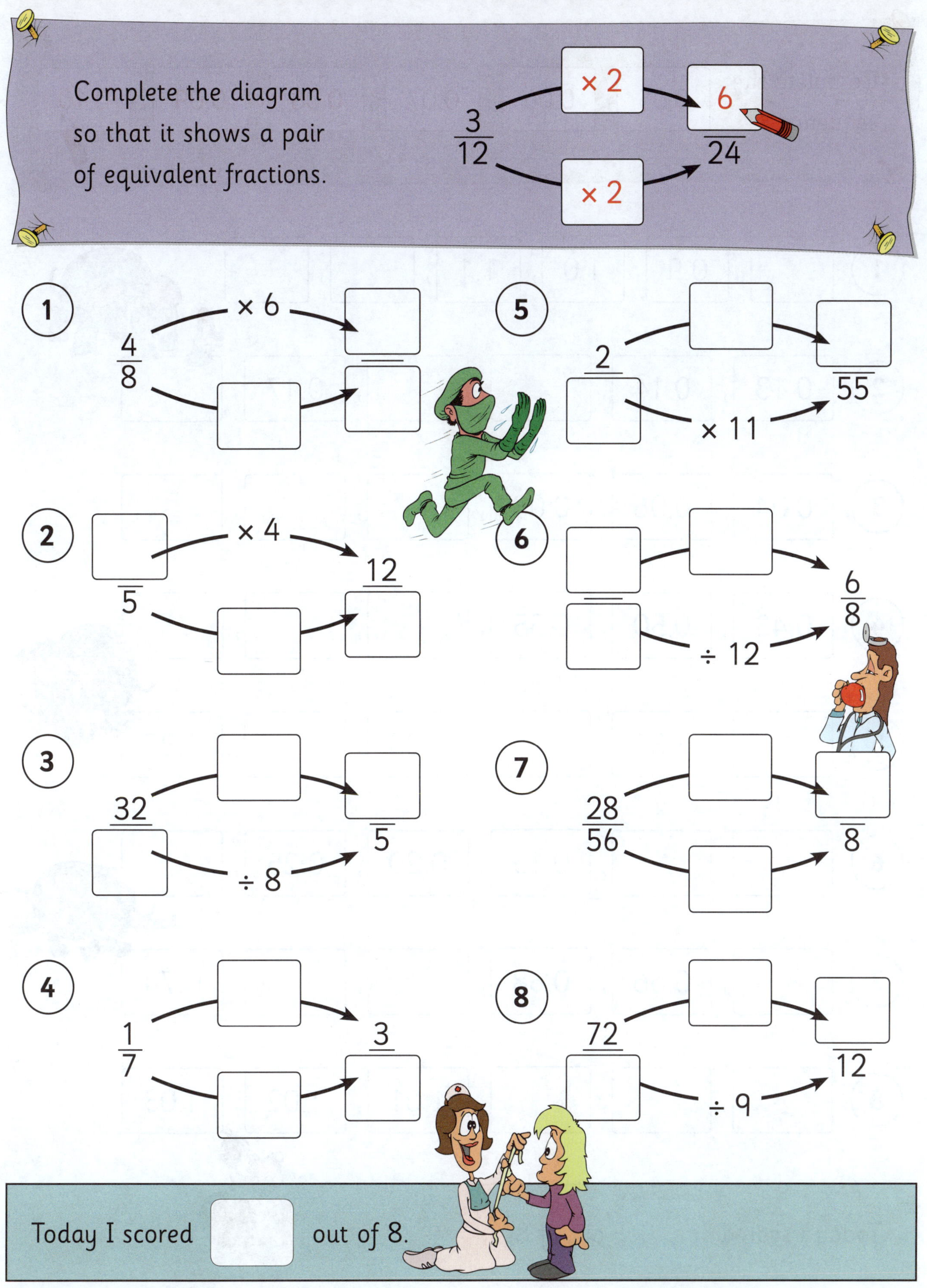

Today I scored [ ] out of 8.

Week 4 — Day 1

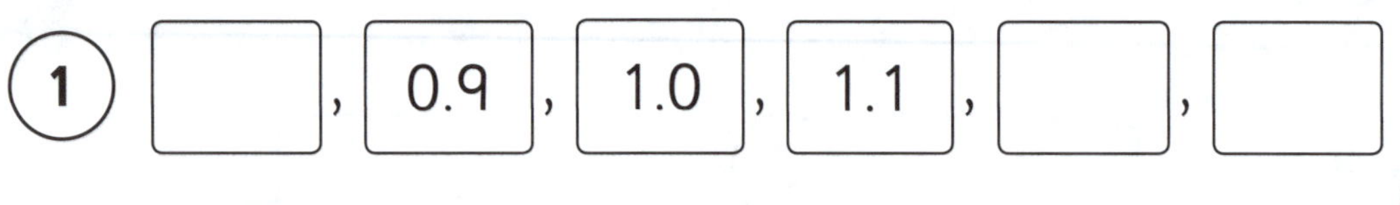

Complete the sequence.

0.05 , 0.06 , 0.07 , 0.08 , 0.09 , 0.10

1)   [ ] , 0.9 , 1.0 , 1.1 , [ ] , [ ]

2)   0.13 , 0.14 , [ ] , [ ] , 0.17 , [ ]

3)   0.04 , 0.06 , 0.08 , [ ] , [ ] , [ ]

4)   0.45 , 0.50 , 0.55 , [ ] , [ ] , [ ]

5)   [ ] , 1.31 , [ ] , 1.33 , [ ] , 1.35

6)   [ ] , [ ] , 0.15 , 0.20 , 0.25 , [ ]

7)   [ ] , 0.66 , 0.68 , [ ] , [ ] , 0.74

8)   [ ] , [ ] , [ ] , 1.01 , 1.02 , 1.03

Today I scored [ ] out of 8.

Week 4 — Day 2

Draw hands on the clock face to show the correct time.

03 : 25

1 05 : 11

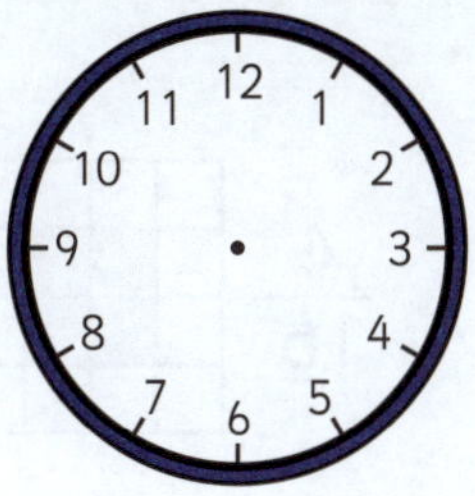

2 10 : 22

3 14 : 55

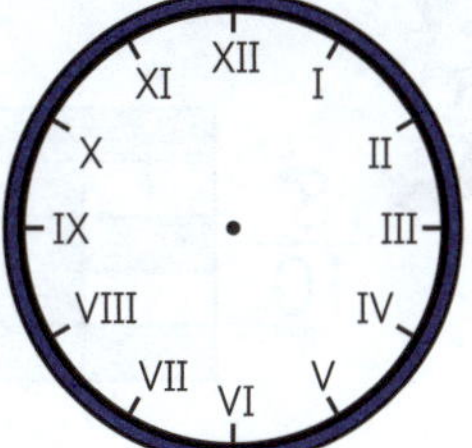

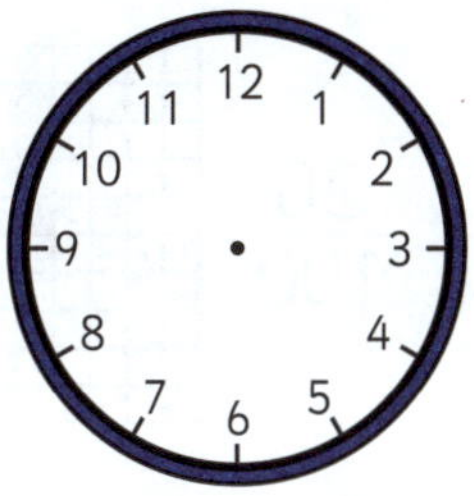

4 17 : 40

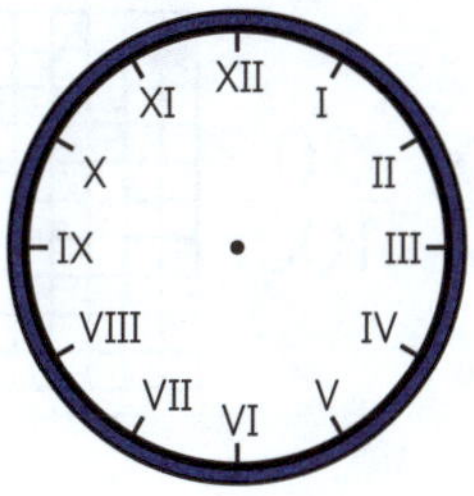

5 13 : 02

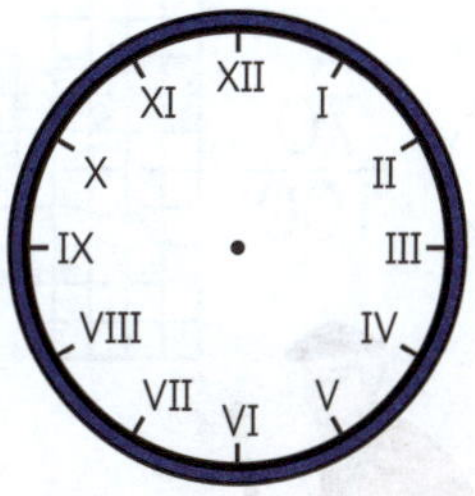

6 19 : 31

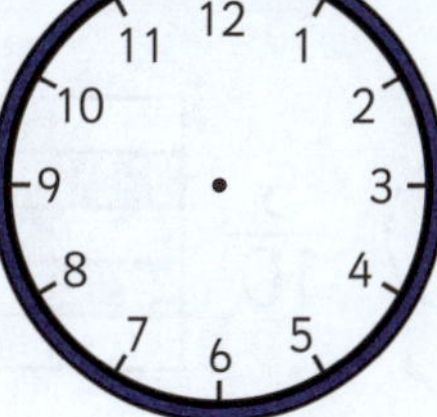

7 18 : 08

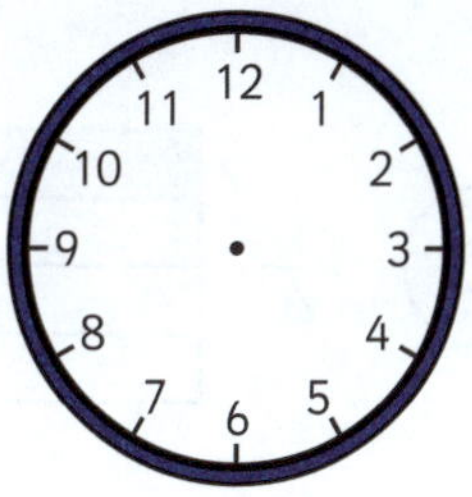

8 13 : 59

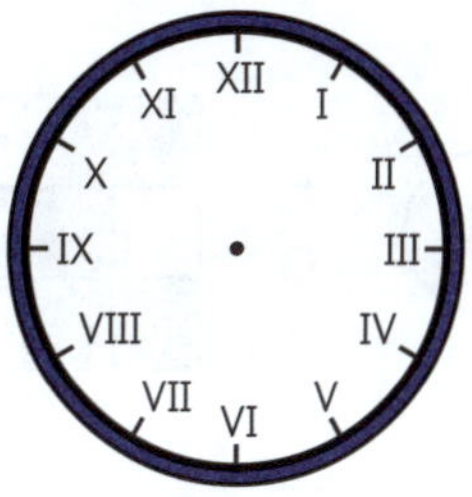

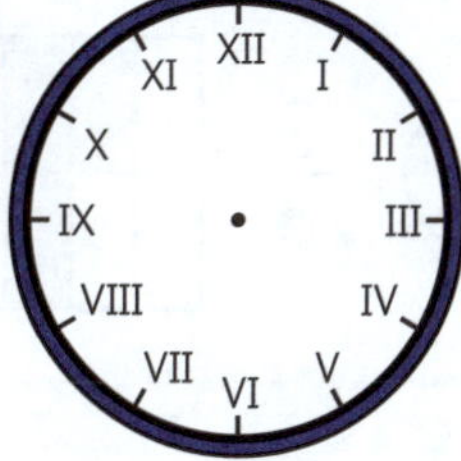

9 16 : 41

10 20 : 48

Today I scored [ ] out of 10.

Year 4 Maths — Summer Term

Week 4 — Day 3

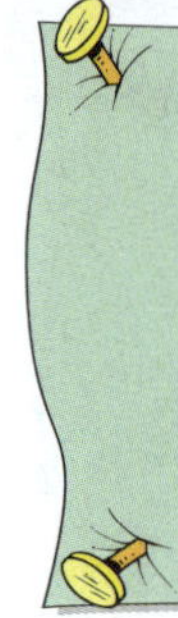

One shape is shaded. Shade the same amount of the second shape and use it to write the equivalent fraction to the one given.

$\frac{6}{10}$ 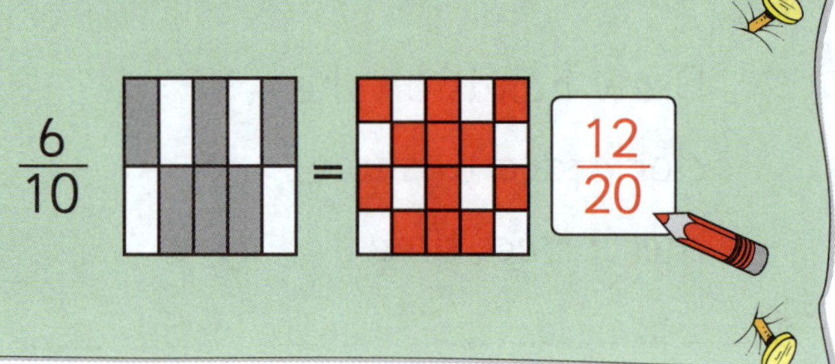 $\frac{12}{20}$

1) $\frac{5}{10}$  = 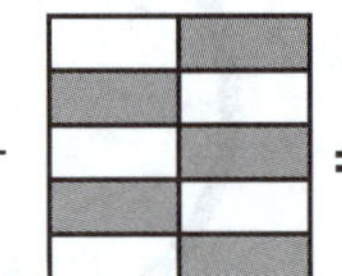 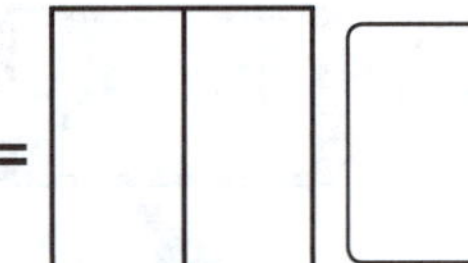

6) $\frac{4}{16}$  = 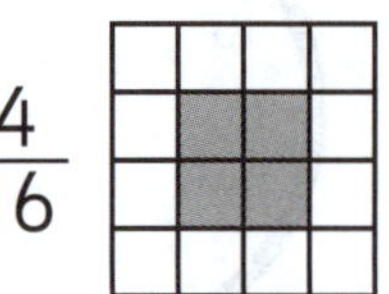 

2) $\frac{1}{4}$ 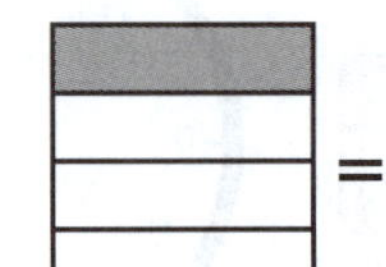 = 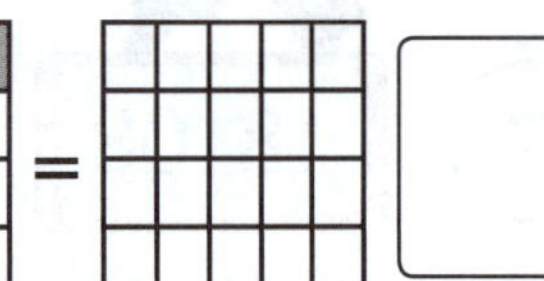 

7) $\frac{8}{10}$ 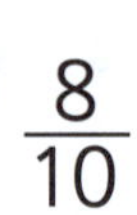 = 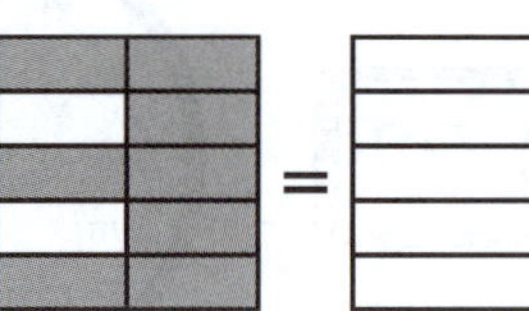 

3) $\frac{6}{9}$ 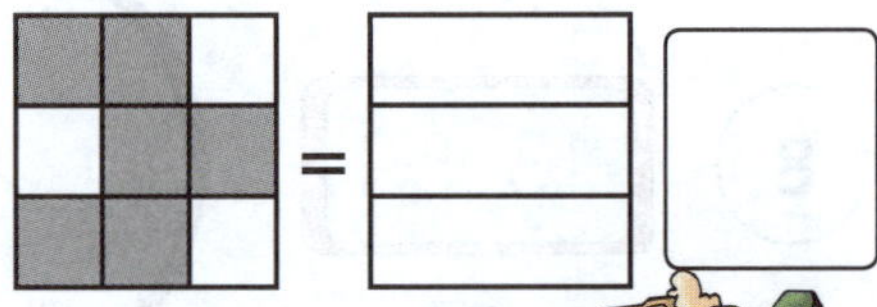

8) $\frac{30}{100}$ 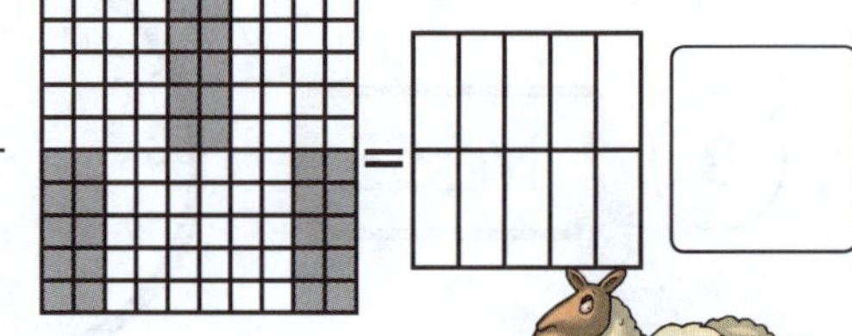

4) $\frac{3}{8}$ 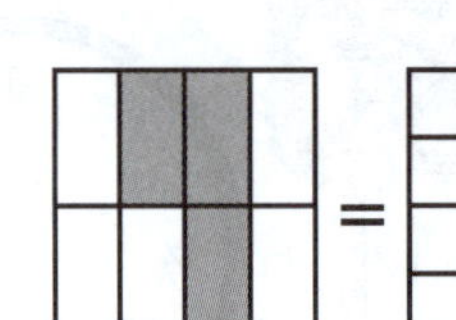

9) $\frac{20}{100}$ 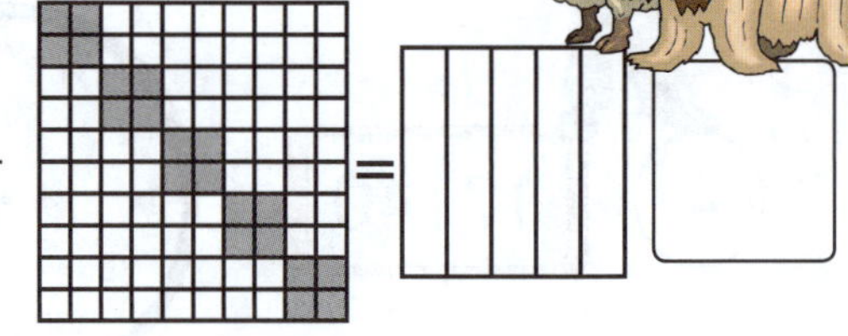

5) $\frac{2}{5}$ 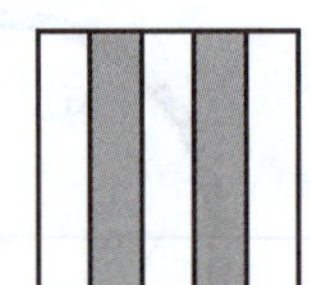

10) $\frac{70}{100}$ 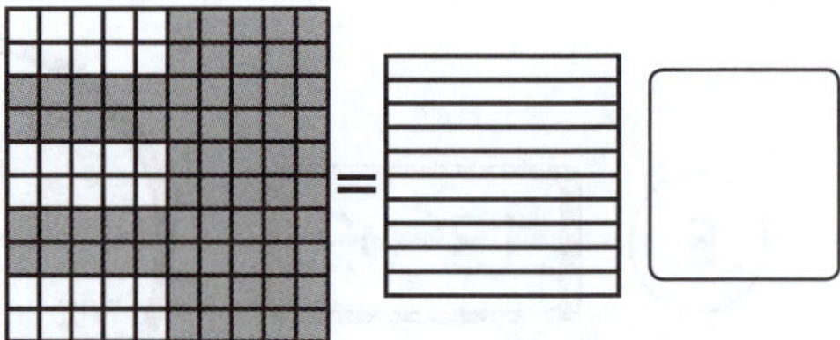

Today I scored ⬚ out of 10.

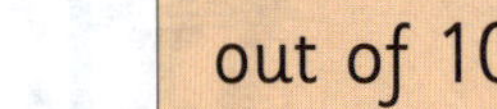

Week 4 — Day 4

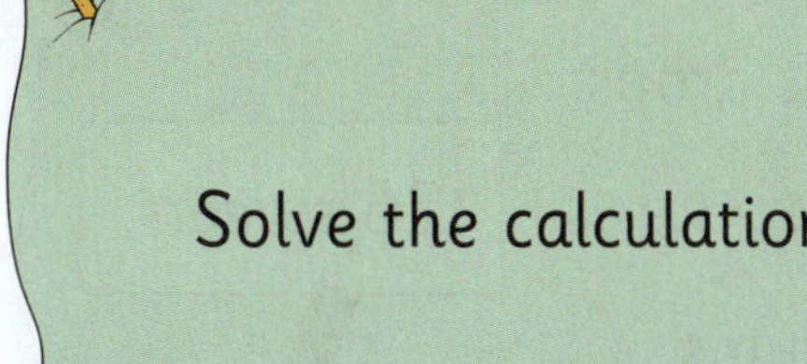

Solve the calculation.

$4352 + 2355 = $ 6707

$$\begin{array}{r} 4352 \\ + \ 2355 \\ \hline 6707 \\ \hline {\scriptstyle 1} \end{array}$$

1) $1678 + 1190 = $

6) $9618 - 7632 = $

2) $3984 + 2374 = $

7) $4414 + 1788 = $

3) $9481 - 7640 = $

8) $7660 - 4697 = $

4) $4706 + 3819 = $

9) $7054 - 2099 = $

5) $5192 - 2244 = $

10) $6538 + 3982 = $

Today I scored ☐ out of 10.

Year 4 Maths — Summer Term

Week 4 — Day 5

How many sweets did the group eat? Darren and his friends have 28 mint drops and 22 lime gums. They eat $\frac{4}{7}$ of the mint drops and $\frac{5}{11}$ of the lime gums.

1. Jemima and her friends have 32 strawberry bottles and 18 cola straws. They eat $\frac{1}{4}$ of the strawberry bottles and $\frac{2}{3}$ of the cola straws.

sweets

2. Faisal and his friends have 21 cherry sherbets and 36 lemon laces. They eat $\frac{2}{3}$ of the cherry sherbets and $\frac{5}{6}$ of the lemon laces.

sweets

3. Siobhan and her friends have 48 coffee drops and 20 chocolate mints. They eat $\frac{7}{8}$ of the coffee drops and $\frac{2}{5}$ of the chocolate mints.

sweets

4. Luke and his friends have 56 honeycomb crunches and 15 orange gums. They eat $\frac{5}{8}$ of the honeycomb crunches and $\frac{4}{5}$ of the orange gums.

sweets

5. Isa and her friends have 72 pear drops and 44 apple straws. They eat $\frac{5}{9}$ of the pear drops and $\frac{6}{11}$ of the apple straws.

sweets

6. Sofia and her friends have 63 kiwi fizzes and 132 mango laces. They eat $\frac{7}{9}$ of the kiwi fizzes and $\frac{7}{12}$ of the mango laces.

sweets

Today I scored ☐ out of 6.

Week 5 — Day 1

Write a calculation you could use to check the answer to the calculation given.

9091 − 5886 = 3205

To check: **3205 + 5886**

1) 8278 − 6358 = 1920

To check:

2) 3037 + 4775 = 7812

To check:

3) 7151 − 2827 = 4324

To check:

4) 1301 + 7946 = 9247

To check:

5) 60.8 − 20.4 = 40.4

To check:

6) 3939 + 5282 = 9221

To check:

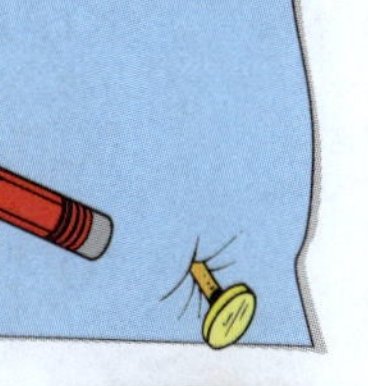

7) 5821 − 1667 = 4154

To check:

8) 26.4 + 30.5 = 56.9

To check:

9) 6449 − 4495 = 1954

To check:

10) 80.6 + 17.5 = 98.1

To check:

11) 77.6 − 57.8 = 19.8

To check:

12) 8643 = 6919 + 1724

To check:

Today I scored [ ] out of 12.

Year 4 Maths — Summer Term

Week 5 — Day 2

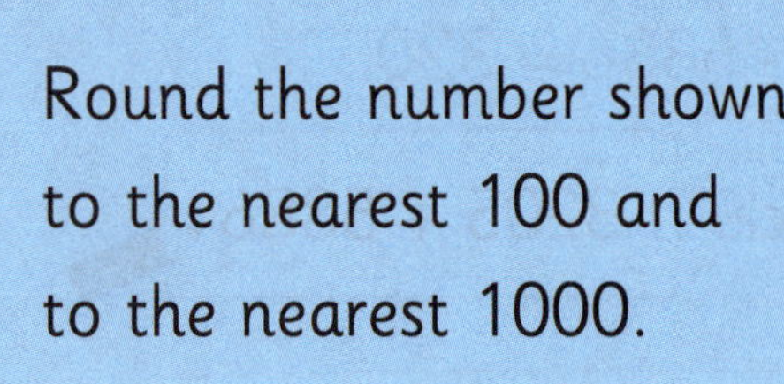

Round the number shown to the nearest 100 and to the nearest 1000.

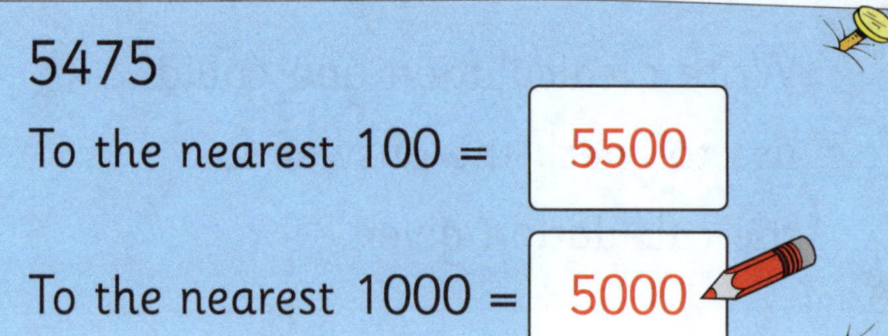

5475
To the nearest 100 = 5500
To the nearest 1000 = 5000

1 4084
To the nearest 100 =
To the nearest 1000 =

2 3530
To the nearest 100 =
To the nearest 1000 =

3 7151
To the nearest 100 =
To the nearest 1000 =

4 9243
To the nearest 100 =
To the nearest 1000 =

5 6698
To the nearest 100 =
To the nearest 1000 =

6 8767
To the nearest 100 =
To the nearest 1000 =

7 2309
To the nearest 100 =
To the nearest 1000 =

8 1826
To the nearest 100 =
To the nearest 1000 =

9 912
To the nearest 100 =
To the nearest 1000 =

10 7489
To the nearest 100 =
To the nearest 1000 =

Today I scored ☐ out of 10.

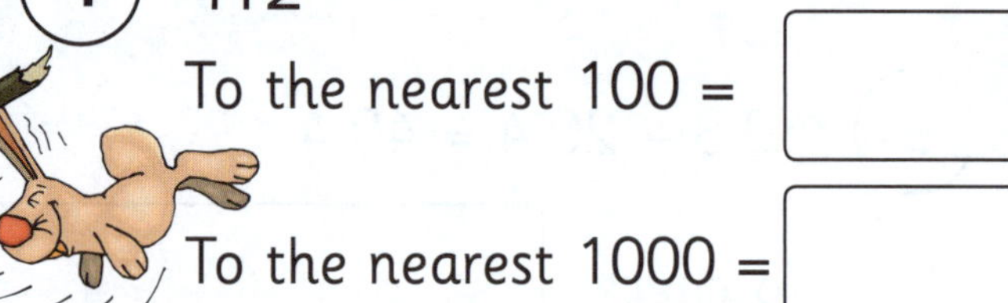

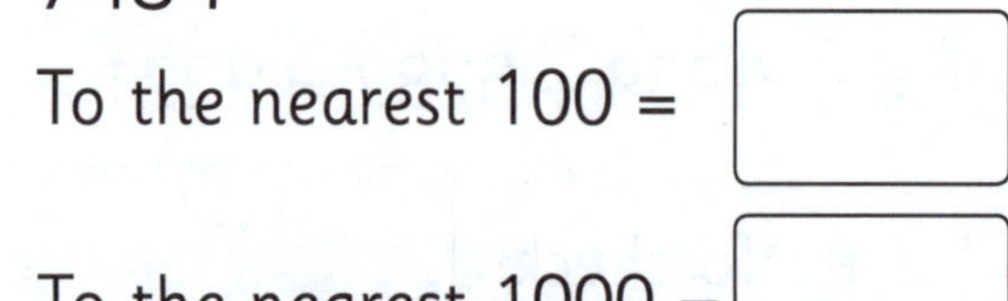

Week 5 — Day 3

How many objects could the person have? Circle all the possible numbers.

Letitia has 60 magnets to the nearest 10.

65   (61)   (59)   53   (63) 

1 Amelia has 40 cuddly toys to the nearest 10.

34   46   42   37   35

2 William has 80 coloured pens to the nearest 10.

84   78   87   72   76

3 Helen has 70 books to the nearest 10.

66   72   61   78   75

4 Rupert has 20 bags to the nearest 10.

16   26   12   23   19

5 Klaus has 30 games to the nearest 10.

23   25   34   39   28

6 Danielle has 50 dresses to the nearest 10.

44   51   57   47   54

7 Charlie has 60 comics to the nearest 10.

51   69   55   64   54

8 Ed has 90 toy cars to the nearest 10.

92   89   86   95   82

9 Jun has 10 teddy bears to the nearest 10.

7   18   15   14   4

10 Kirsty has 100 caps to the nearest 10.

93   97   101   106   98

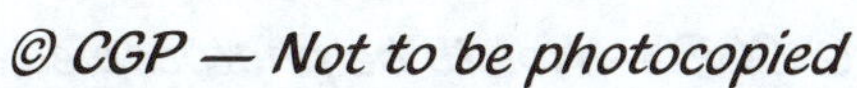

Today I scored ☐ out of 10.

Year 4 Maths — Summer Term

Week 5 — Day 4

How long did the person spend doing the activity?

Iliya went cycling in the forest. He paid £10 for some knee pads, £15 per day to hire a bike and £5 per day to hire a helmet. He paid £70 in total.

3 days

1 Leona went on a skiing holiday. She paid £5 for some ski socks, £9 per day to hire some skis and £3 per day to hire some ski boots. She paid £125 in total.

☐ days

2 Roy went on a fishing holiday. He paid £4 to park his car, £5 per day to hire a fishing rod and £3 per day to hire a fishing net. He paid £52 in total.

☐ days

3 Darcie went ice-skating. She paid £3 to use a locker, £6 per hour to hire some ice skates and £5 per hour to hire a push-along penguin. She paid £25 in total.

☐ hours

4 Josh went rollerblading at the skate park. He paid £6 for admission, £4 per hour to hire some rollerblades and £3 per hour to hire a helmet. He paid £34 in total.

☐ hours

5 Alison went horse-riding at the farm. She paid £11 for some riding gloves, £31 per hour for the use of a horse and £9 per hour for an instructor. She paid £91 in total.

☐ hours

Today I scored ☐ out of 5.

Week 5 — Day 5

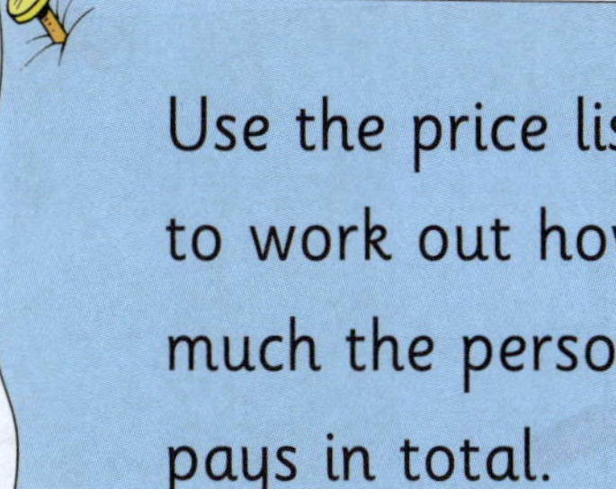

Use the price list to work out how much the person pays in total.

Oranges	35p each
Pasties	85p each
Cauliflowers	70p each
Onions	50p each

Shohidul buys two oranges, one cauliflower and three onions.

£2.90

1

Nectarines	45p each
Yoghurts	90p each
Bananas	40p each
Bread rolls	55p each

Nigella buys two yoghurts, one bread roll and one nectarine.

£

2

Leeks	25p each
Coconuts	65p each
Mangoes	80p each
Kiwis	30p each

Jung buys one coconut, two mangoes and three kiwis.

£

3

Fishcakes	85p each
Meatballs	40p each
Avocados	90p each
Cakes	55p each

Vanessa buys two fishcakes, five meatballs and two avocados.

£

4

Beef patties	95p each
Lemons	35p each
Peppers	40p each
Peaches	45p each

Gertrude buys two beef patties, one peach and three peppers.

£

5

Mushrooms	40p each
Limes	30p each
Cabbages	75p each
Cucumbers	65p each

Rajah buys four mushrooms, one cabbage and three cucumbers.

£

Today I scored [ ] out of 5.

Year 4 Maths — Summer Term

Week 6 — Day 1

The coordinates of a shape's vertices are given. Plot the points and draw the shape on the grid.

(1, 1)
(1, 4)
(4, 4)
(4, 1)

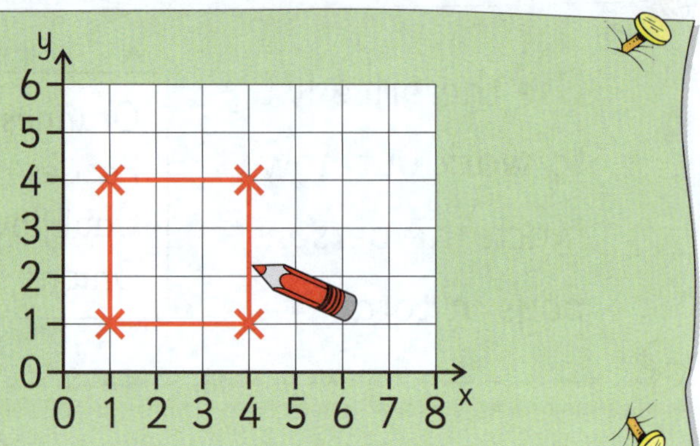

1

(1, 5)
(6, 3)
(1, 1)

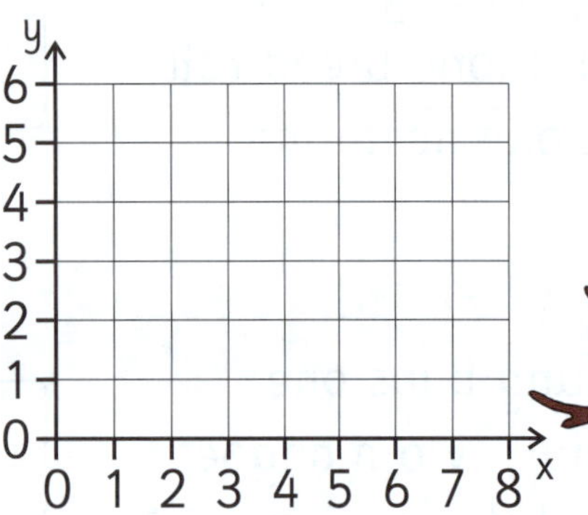

2

(1, 2)
(4, 5)
(7, 2)

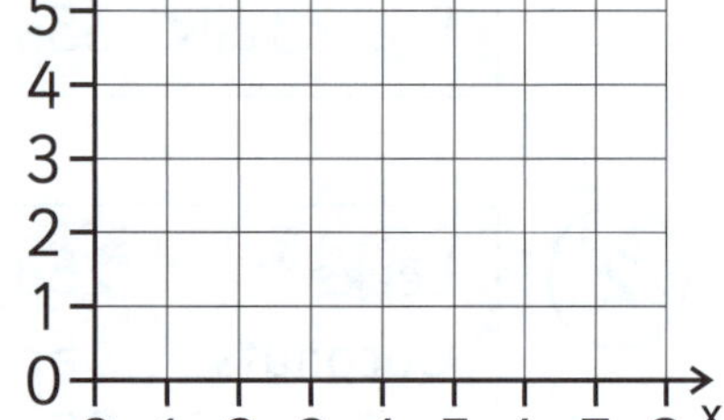

3

(8, 2)
(8, 5)
(3, 5)
(3, 2)

4

(0, 0)
(0, 5)
(5, 5)
(5, 0)

5

(2, 3)
(8, 3)
(6, 1)
(0, 1)

6

(7, 5)
(5, 4)
(3, 1)
(7, 3)

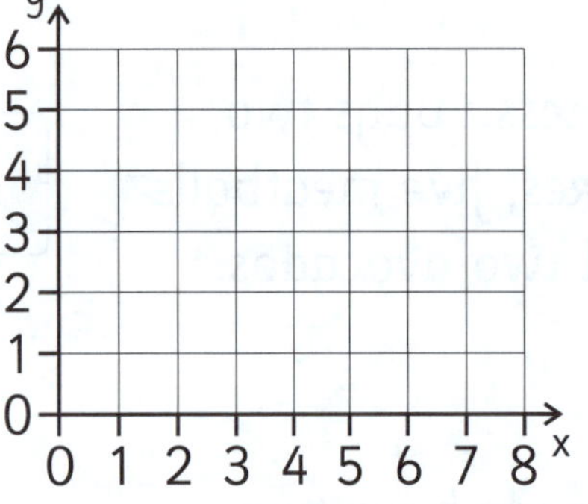
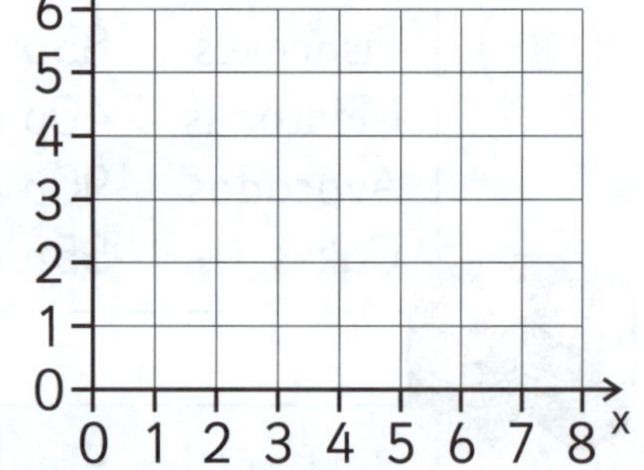
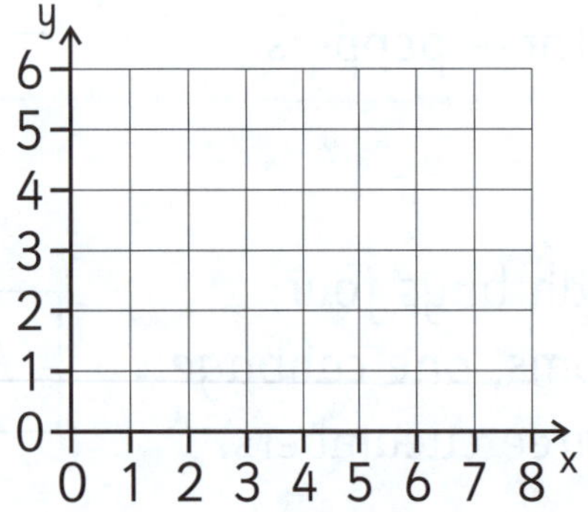
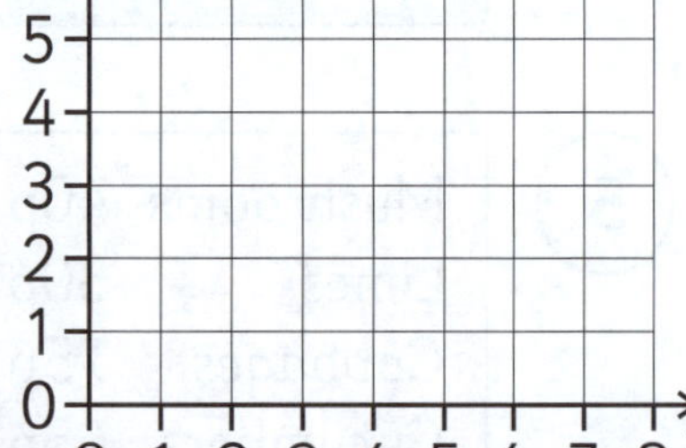

Today I scored [ ] out of 6.

Week 6 — Day 2

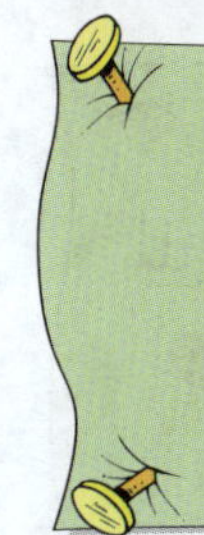

Solve the calculation.

$4 \times 2 \times 6 = \boxed{48}$

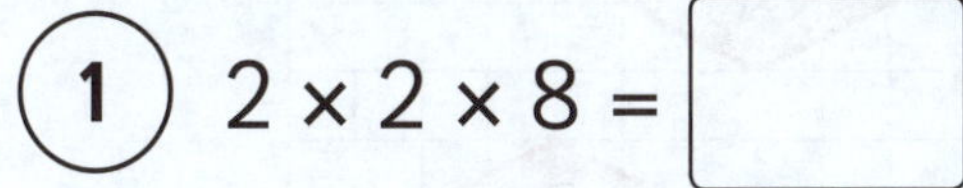

1 $2 \times 2 \times 8 = \boxed{}$

2 $3 \times 5 \times 3 = \boxed{}$

3 $10 \times 4 \times 3 = \boxed{}$

4 $3 \times 4 \times 5 = \boxed{}$

5 $11 \times 2 \times 5 = \boxed{}$

6 $3 \times 12 \times 3 = \boxed{}$

7 $4 \times 7 \times 2 = \boxed{}$

8 $2 \times 7 \times 6 = \boxed{}$

9 $2 \times 11 \times 6 = \boxed{}$

10 $4 \times 9 \times 10 = \boxed{}$

11 $5 \times 3 \times 8 = \boxed{}$

12 $5 \times 6 \times 5 = \boxed{}$

Today I scored $\boxed{}$ out of 12.

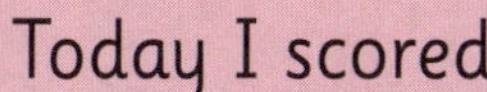
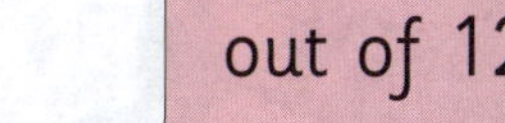

Year 4 Maths — Summer Term

Week 6 — Day 3

Shape A has been translated to give shape B. Fill in the boxes to describe the translation.

5 squares **right** and **3** squares **down** .

1

___ squares ___ and ___ squares ___ .

2

___ squares ___ and ___ squares ___ .

3

___ squares ___ and ___ squares ___ .

4

___ squares ___ and ___ squares ___ .

5

___ squares ___ and ___ squares ___ .

6

___ squares ___ and ___ squares ___ .

Today I scored ___ out of 6.

Week 6 — Day 4

What fraction of their original amount does the person have left over?

Lizzie has £13. She spends £2 on matches and £6 on a candle.

Fraction left over = $\frac{5}{13}$

1 Daniya has £25. She spends £10 on a lamp and £4 on a light bulb.

Fraction left over =

2 Jack has £17. He spends £3 on some pencils and £11 on a notebook.

Fraction left over =

3 Lee has £58. He spends £13 on a blanket and £24 on some cushions.

Fraction left over =

4 Debbie has £45. She spends £21 on a vase and £11 on some flowers.

Fraction left over =

5 Brenda has £64. She spends £12 on a plant and £17 on a watering can.

Fraction left over =

6 Aggrey has £181. He spends £52 on a golf club and £16 on some balls.

Fraction left over =

7 Isla has £128. She spends £35 on a video game and £34 on some DVDs.

Fraction left over =

8 Dave has £205. He spends £27 on a canvas and £29 on some oil paints.

Fraction left over =

Today I scored [ ] out of 8.

Year 4 Maths — Summer Term

Week 6 — Day 5

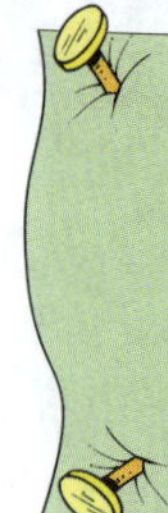

Add up the measurements to give the total in the correct units.

$4.5 \text{ km} + 300 \text{ m} + 200 \text{ cm} =$ **4802** m

1) $1.6 \text{ m} + 100 \text{ cm} =$ ____ cm

2) $12 \text{ cm} + 9 \text{ mm} =$ ____ mm

3) $650 \text{ g} + 6 \text{ kg} =$ ____ g 

4) $6.3 \text{ l} + 2500 \text{ ml} =$ ____ ml

5) $8.1 \text{ kg} + 550 \text{ g} =$ ____ g

6) $6 \text{ m} + 300 \text{ cm} + 10 \text{ mm} =$ ____ cm

7) $3.2 \text{ m} + 250 \text{ cm} + 100 \text{ mm} =$ ____ cm

8) $5.5 \text{ km} + 900 \text{ m} + 200 \text{ cm} =$ ____ m 

9) $800 \text{ cm} + 0.7 \text{ km} + 73 \text{ m} =$ ____ m

10) $927 \text{ m} + 500 \text{ cm} + 1.4 \text{ km} =$ ____ m

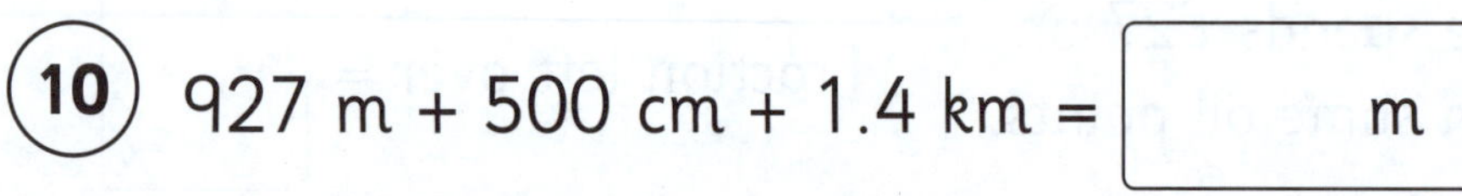

Today I scored ____ out of 10.

Week 7 — Day 1

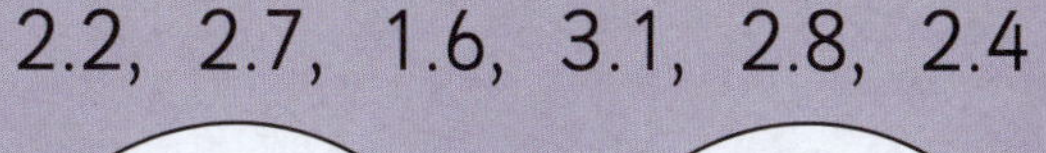

Round the decimals to the nearest whole number and write them in the correct circle.

2.2, 2.7, 1.6, 3.1, 2.8, 2.4

2.2
2
2.4   1.6

3.1
2.8
3
2.7

1   3.6, 4.4, 5.3, 4.6, 5.4, 4.1

4

5

4   7.6, 8.4, 8.2, 9.3, 8.5, 8.1

8

9

2   6.4, 6.6, 7.2, 6.7, 6.5, 6.3

6

7

5   1.3, 1.9, 1.5, 0.8, 2.3, 1.4

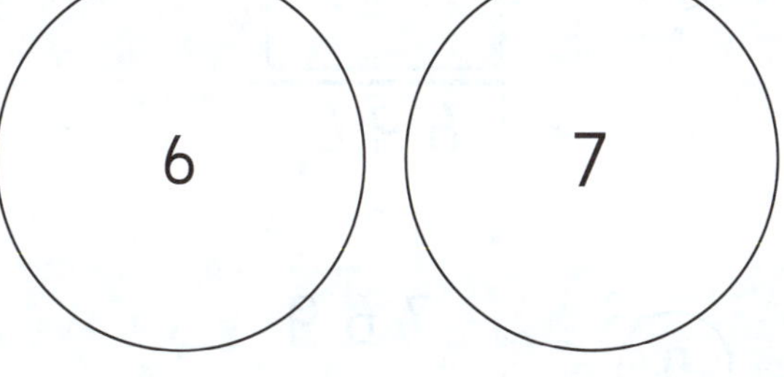

1

2

3   9.8, 9.5, 8.7, 9.9, 10.2, 9.2

9

10

6   0.1, 1.2, 0.4, 0.2, 0.5, 0.6

0

1

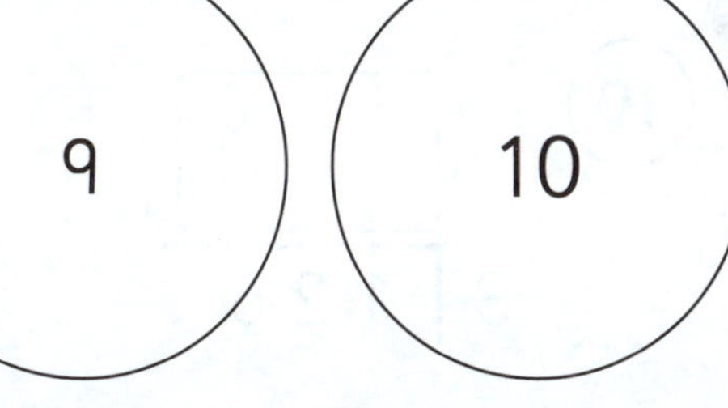

Today I scored [ ] out of 6.

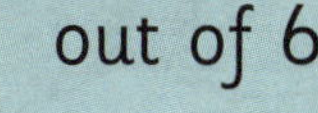

Year 4 Maths — Summer Term

Week 7 — Day 2

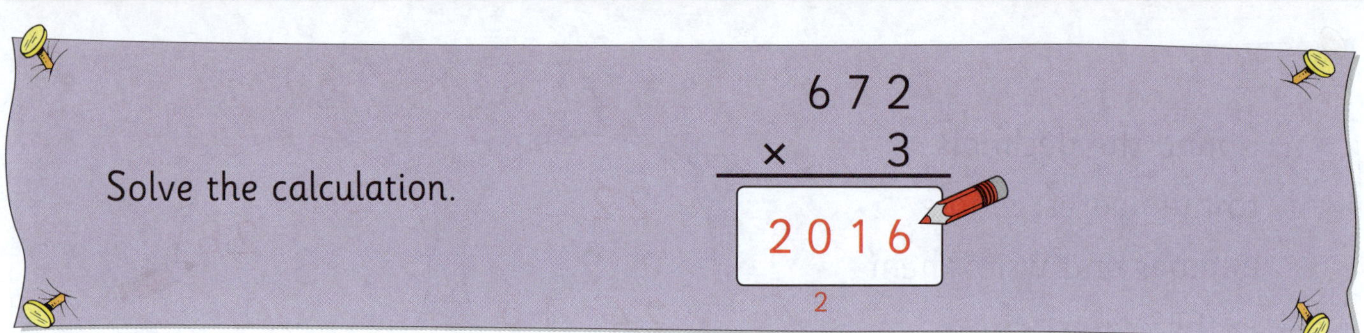

Solve the calculation.

$$\begin{array}{r} 672 \\ \times\ 3 \\ \hline 2016 \\ \end{array}$$

1
$$\begin{array}{r} 213 \\ \times\ 4 \\ \hline \end{array}$$

2
$$\begin{array}{r} 131 \\ \times\ 6 \\ \hline \end{array}$$

3
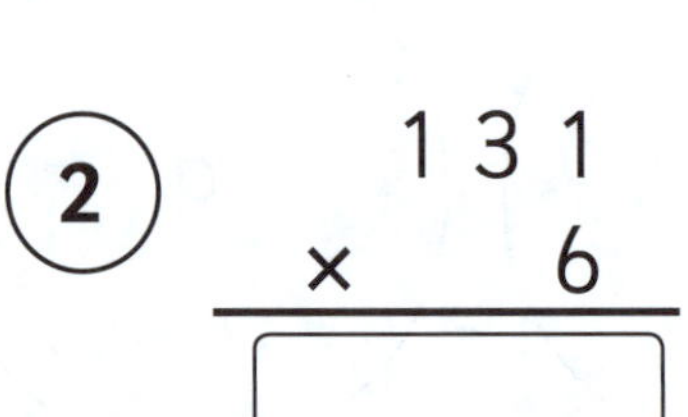
$$\begin{array}{r} 473 \\ \times\ 8 \\ \hline \end{array}$$

4
$$4\ \overline{|\ 816}$$

5
$$\begin{array}{r} 396 \\ \times\ 6 \\ \hline \end{array}$$

6
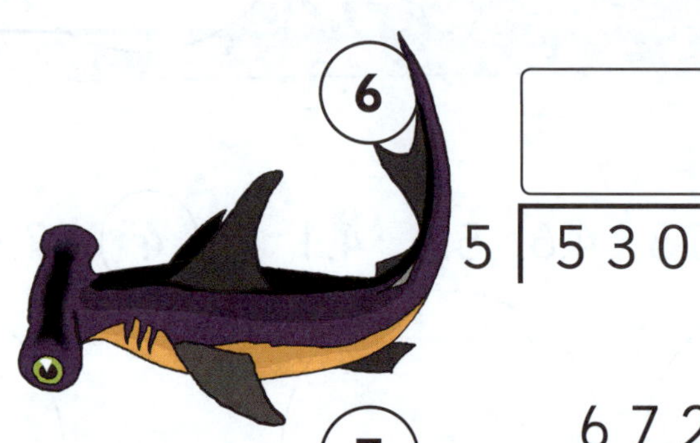
$$5\ \overline{|\ 530}$$

7
$$\begin{array}{r} 672 \\ \times\ 9 \\ \hline \end{array}$$

8
$$6\ \overline{|\ 696}$$

9
$$\begin{array}{r} 769 \\ \times\ 7 \\ \hline \end{array}$$

10
$$3\ \overline{|\ 126}$$

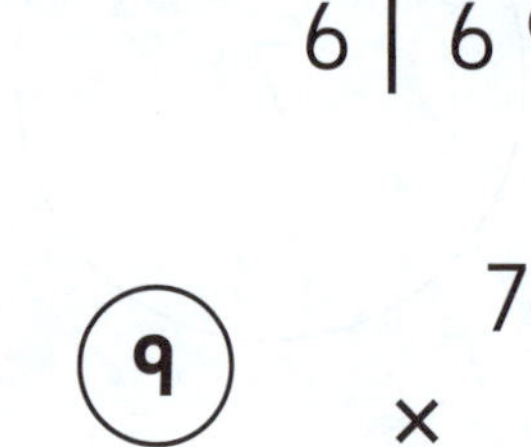

Today I scored ☐ out of 10.

Week 7 — Day 3

Fill in the boxes to complete the addition using partitioning.

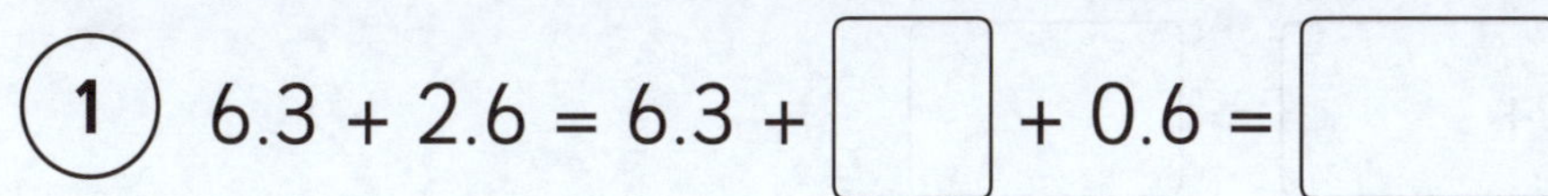

$5.4 + 3.7 = 5.4 + \boxed{3} + 0.7 = \boxed{9.1}$

1) $6.3 + 2.6 = 6.3 + \boxed{} + 0.6 = \boxed{}$

2) $6.5 + 3.3 = 6.5 + 3 + \boxed{} = \boxed{}$

3) $8.4 + 1.5 = 8.4 + \boxed{} + 0.5 = \boxed{}$

4) $6.1 + 1.7 = 6.1 + 1 + \boxed{} = \boxed{}$

5) $16.1 + 3.4 = 16.1 + \boxed{} + 0.4 = \boxed{}$

6) $33.1 + 2.6 = 33.1 + 2 + \boxed{} = \boxed{}$

7) $64 + 5.9 = 64 + \boxed{} + 0.9 = \boxed{}$

8) $56.5 + 26.2 = 56.5 + 20 + \boxed{} + 0.2 = \boxed{}$

9) $31.9 + 25.6 = 31.9 + 20 + \boxed{} + \boxed{} = \boxed{}$

10) $26.5 + 13.8 = 26.5 + \boxed{} + 3 + \boxed{} = \boxed{}$

Today I scored $\boxed{}$ out of 10.

Year 4 Maths — Summer Term

Week 7 — Day 4

Write each fraction as a decimal to complete the calculation.

$\frac{7}{10} + \frac{1}{2} =$ 0.7 + 0.5 = 1.2

1) $\frac{1}{10} + \frac{6}{10} =$ [+] = [ ]

2) $\frac{1}{2} + \frac{1}{10} =$ [+] = [ ]

3) $\frac{1}{4} + \frac{1}{100} =$ [+] = [ ]

4) $\frac{5}{10} + \frac{4}{10} =$ [+] = [ ]

5) $\frac{2}{100} + \frac{3}{4} =$ [+] = [ ]

6) $\frac{4}{100} + \frac{9}{100} =$ [+] = [ ]

7) $\frac{30}{100} + \frac{65}{100} =$ [+] = [ ]

8) $\frac{8}{10} + \frac{1}{2} =$ [+] = [ ]

9) $\frac{3}{10} + \frac{54}{100} =$ [+] = [ ]

10) $\frac{3}{4} + \frac{43}{100} =$ [+] = [ ]

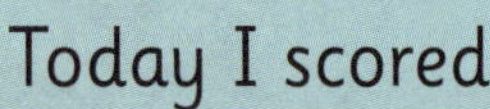 Today I scored [ ] out of 10.

Week 7 — Day 5

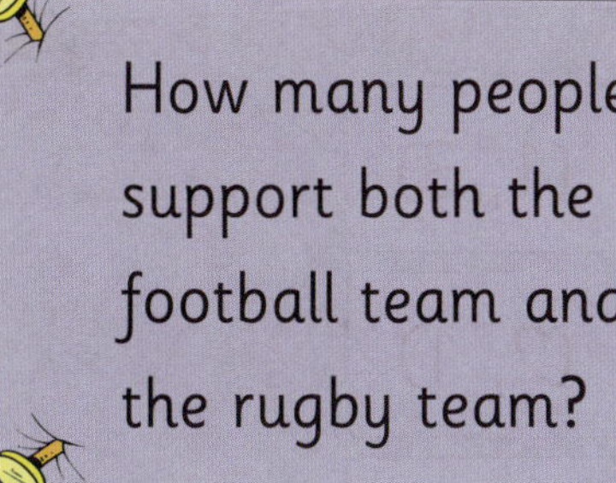

How many people support both the football team and the rugby team?

Puddleton's football and rugby teams have 188 supporters in total. 120 people support the football team and 92 support the rugby team.

24 people

1. Diggleby's football and rugby teams have 200 supporters in total. 125 people support the football team and 112 support the rugby team.

______ people

2. Lampford's football and rugby teams have 409 supporters in total. 270 people support the football team and 247 support the rugby team.

______ people

3. Crinock's football and rugby teams have 322 supporters in total. 158 people support the football team and 189 support the rugby team.

______ people

4. Raddlebury's football and rugby teams have 620 supporters in total. 402 people support the football team and 319 support the rugby team.

______ people

5. Illerbridge's football and rugby teams have 864 supporters in total. 641 people support the football team and 471 support the rugby team.

______ people

6. Craggstrath's football and rugby teams have 622 supporters in total. 438 people support the football team and 571 support the rugby team.

______ people

Today I scored [ ] out of 6.

Year 4 Maths — Summer Term

Week 8 — Day 1

Look at the grid. Write down the coordinates of each point.

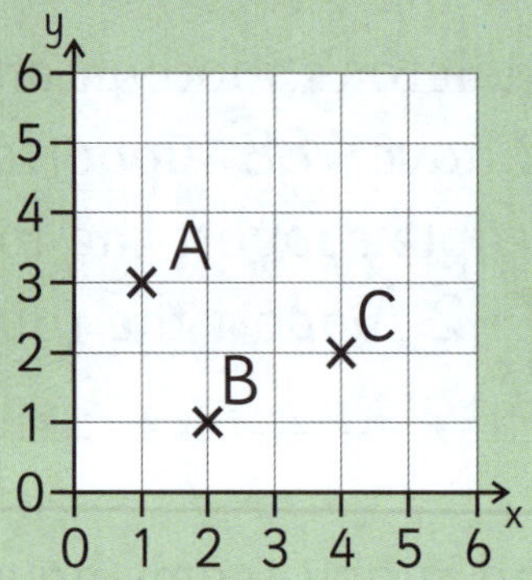

A = **(1, 3)**

B = **(2, 1)**

C = **(4, 2)**

1 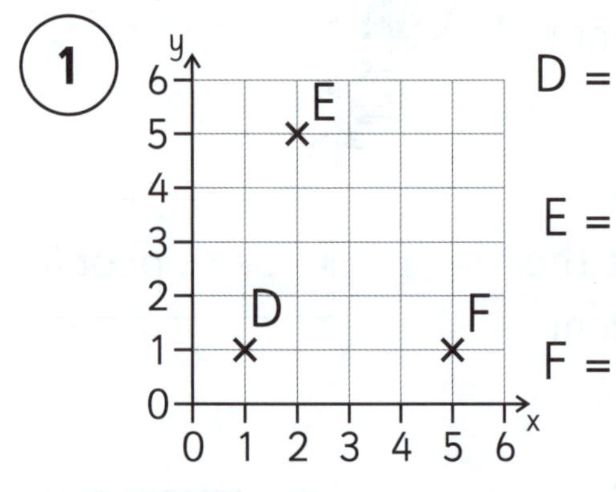

D =

E =

F =

2 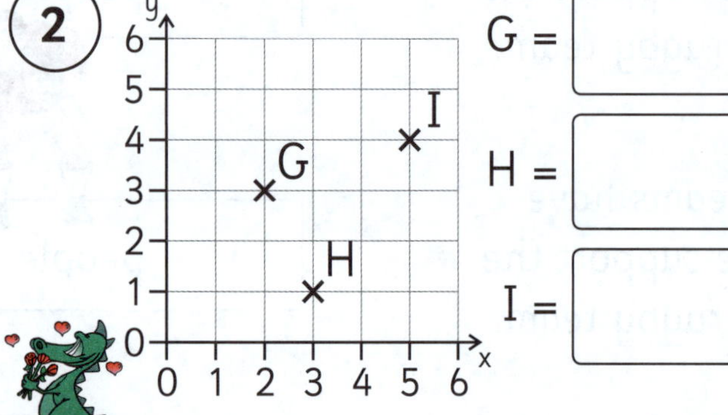

G =

H =

I =

3 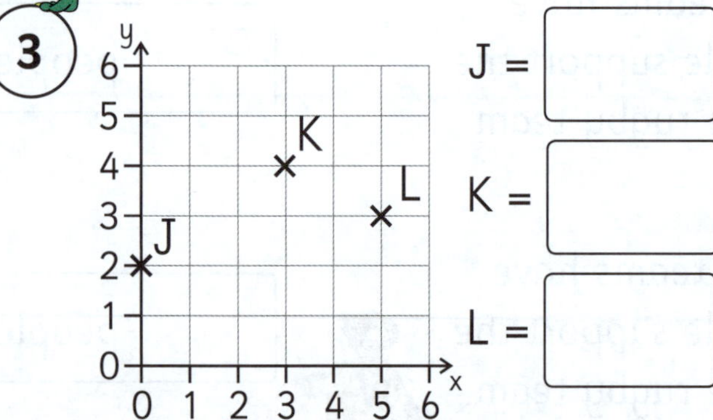

J =

K =

L =

4 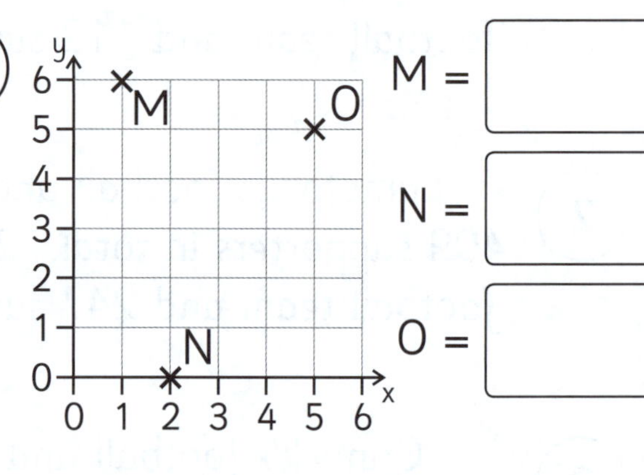

M =

N =

O =

5 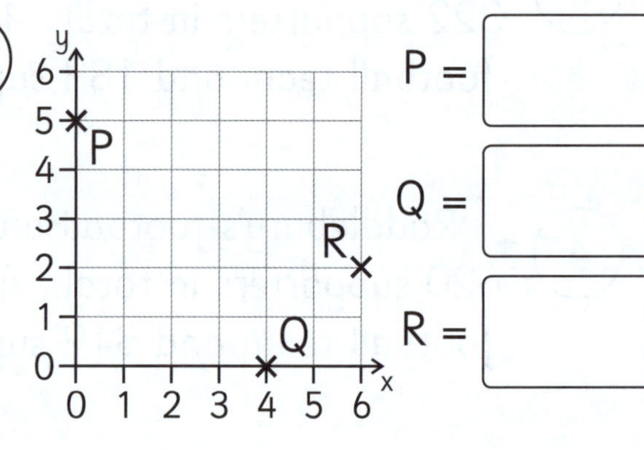

P =

Q =

R =

6 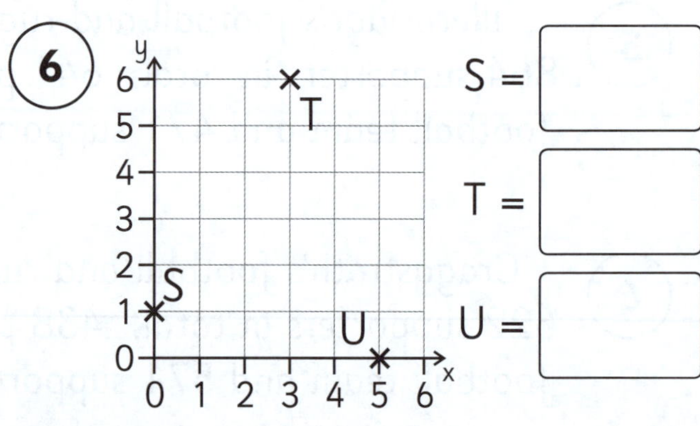

S =

T =

U =

Today I scored [ ] out of 6.

Week 8 — Day 2

Circle the values in the box that match the description.

Volumes more than 3.62 l.

(4.63 l) 3.42 l 3.60 l (3.97 l) 3.27 l

1	Lengths longer than 23.56 m.	24.56 m	22.67 m	23.57 m	23.23 m	23.66 m
2	Volumes less than 5.40 ml.	4.50 ml	5.42 ml	5.04 ml	5.34 ml	5.49 ml
3	Weights heavier than 66.27 kg.	66.19 kg	67.26 kg	65.97 kg	66.72 kg	68.25 kg
4	Weights heavier than 115.31 g.	151.30 g	15.32 g	115.29 g	115.47 g	115.17 g
5	Weights lighter than 6.89 kg.	6.98 kg	7.69 kg	5.91 kg	6.79 kg	6.92 kg
6	Lengths shorter than 4.34 cm.	4.47 cm	4.24 cm	3.35 cm	4.43 cm	4.05 cm
7	Volumes less than 56.78 l.	56.77 l	57.67 l	55.89 l	56.87 l	56.69 l
8	Weights lighter than 17.09 g.	16.17 g	17.90 g	17.11 g	17.07 g	16.99 g
9	Lengths longer than 10.85 m.	11.95 m	10.78 m	10.79 m	10.08 m	10.99 m
10	Volumes more than 296.66 l.	296.61 l	296.95 l	296.76 l	296.59 l	295.99 l

Today I scored [ ] out of 10.

Year 4 Maths — Summer Term

Week 8 — Day 3

Work out the perimeter of the shape.

1. 13 m / 6 m / 6 m / 6 m / 6 m / 13 m — ___ m

2. 4 m / 9 m / 4 m / 9 m / 9 m / 12 m — ___ m

3. 6 m / 6 m / 7 m / 6 m / 4 m / 7 m / 6 m / 6 m — ___ m

4. 7 m / 7 m / 14 m / 8 m / 7 m / 8 m / 7 m / 14 m / 7 m — ___ m

5. 16 m / 12 m / 17 m / 12 m / 12 m / 12 m — ___ m

6. 21 m / 11 m / 11 m / 7 m / 4 m / 9 m / 9 m / 20 m — ___ m

7. 18 m / 19 m / 8 m / 17 m / 17 m / 21 m / 15 m — ___ m

8. 29 m / 11 m / 23 m / 11 m / 9 m / 13 m / 12 m / 18 m — ___ m

Today I scored ___ out of 8.

Week 8 — Day 4

Work out how many minutes of the film the person has left to watch.

Scott is watching a film that is 210 minutes long. He watches $\frac{1}{3}$ of the film on Monday and another 62 minutes on Tuesday.

1 Margot is watching a film that is 180 minutes long. She watches $\frac{6}{9}$ of the film before her bath and another 52 minutes after her bath.

minutes

2 Ashton is watching a film that is 160 minutes long. He watches $\frac{3}{4}$ of the film in the morning and another 17 minutes in the evening.

minutes

3 Ava-May is watching a film that is 96 minutes long. She watches $\frac{5}{12}$ of the film on Friday and another 18 minutes on Saturday.

minutes

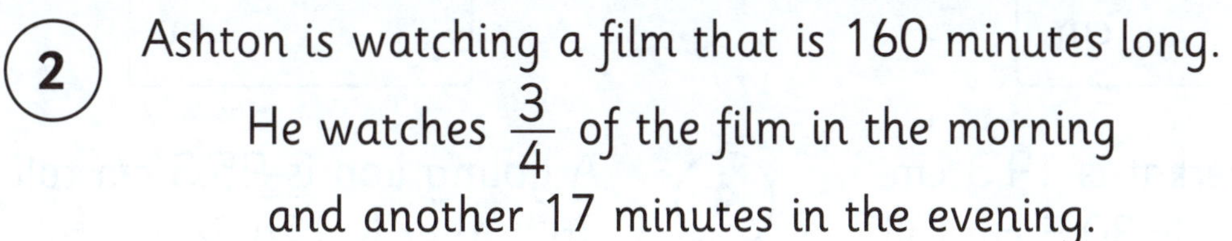

4 Asim is watching a film that is 240 minutes long. He watches $\frac{1}{8}$ of the film before school and another 27 minutes after school.

minutes

5 Jasper is watching a film that is 132 minutes long. He watches $\frac{3}{11}$ of the film on Thursday and another 79 minutes on Friday.

minutes

Today I scored ☐ out of 5.

Week 8 — Day 5

How much taller than the young animal is its parent?

A young cow is 1.11 m tall. Its mother is 1.7 m tall.

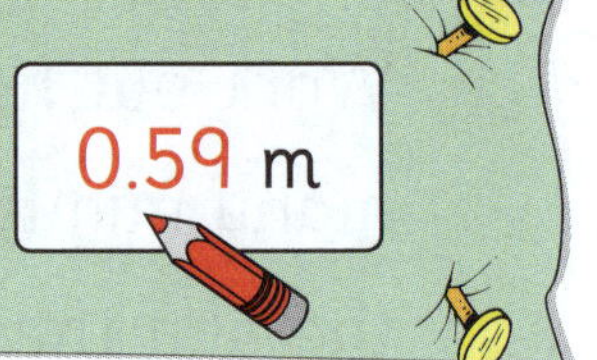

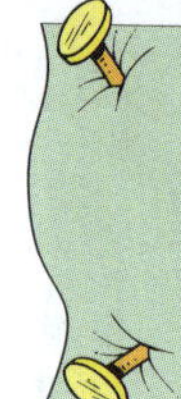

1 A young gorilla is 1.1 m tall. Its father is 1.8 m tall.

m

2 A young penguin is 24.2 cm tall. Its mother is 54.9 cm tall.

cm

3 A young meerkat is 19.3 cm tall. Its father is 30.5 cm tall.

cm

4 A young zebra is 1.09 m tall. Its father is 1.4 m tall.

m

5 A young goat is 67.67 cm tall. Its mother is 89.7 cm tall.

cm

6 A young horse is 0.7 m tall. Its mother is 1.42 m tall.

m

7 A young dog is 560.28 mm tall. Its mother is 881.67 mm tall.

mm

8 A young ostrich is 0.98 m tall. Its mother is 1.67 m tall.

m

9 A young lion is 95.3 cm tall. Its father is 124.34 cm tall.

cm

10 A young swan is 0.79 m tall. Its mother is 1.06 m tall.

m

11 A young pig is 369.7 mm tall. Its mother is 837.32 mm tall.

mm

12 A young bear is 59.26 cm tall. Its father is 100.15 cm tall.

cm

Today I scored ____ out of 12.

Week 9 — Day 1

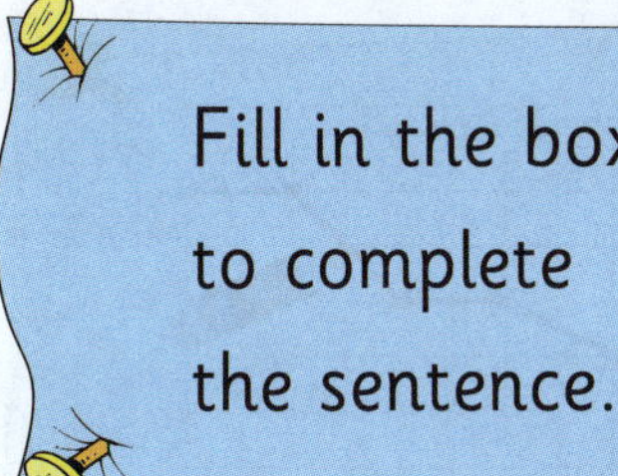

Fill in the box to complete the sentence.

16.4 has a **6** in the ones place.

1 301.45 has a ⬜ in the hundreds place.

2 20.34 has a 2 in the ⬜ place.

3 72.63 has a ⬜ in the hundredths place.

4 31.69 has a ⬜ in the tenths place.

5 847.75 has a ⬜ in the tens place.

6 573.02 has a 0 in the ⬜ place.

7 22.46 has a ⬜ in the ones place.

8 184.15 has a 5 in the ⬜ place.

9 718.74 has a ⬜ in the tenths place.

10 831.65 has an 8 in the ⬜ place.

11 160.44 has a ⬜ in the hundredths place.

12 383.07 has an 8 in the ⬜ place.

Today I scored ⬜ out of 12.

Year 4 Maths — Summer Term

Week 9 — Day 2

The graph shows how far Adam was from home at different times of the day. Use the information to complete the graph.

Adam was at home at 08:00 and was 7 km away at 10:00.

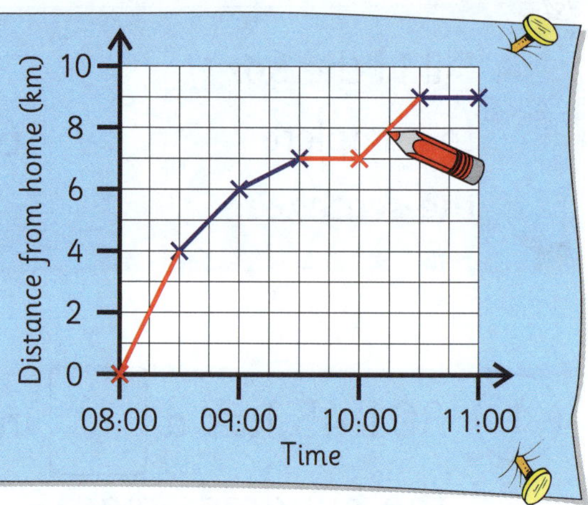

1 Adam was 6 km away from home at 14:00 and was 5 km away at 15:00.

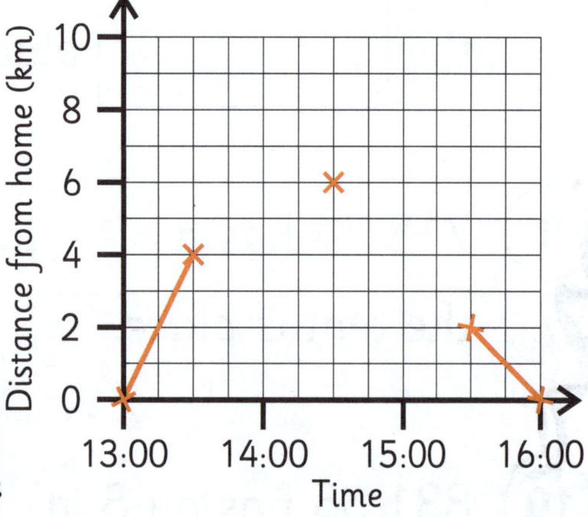

2 Adam was 20 km away from home at 11:00 and was 18 km away at 11:30.

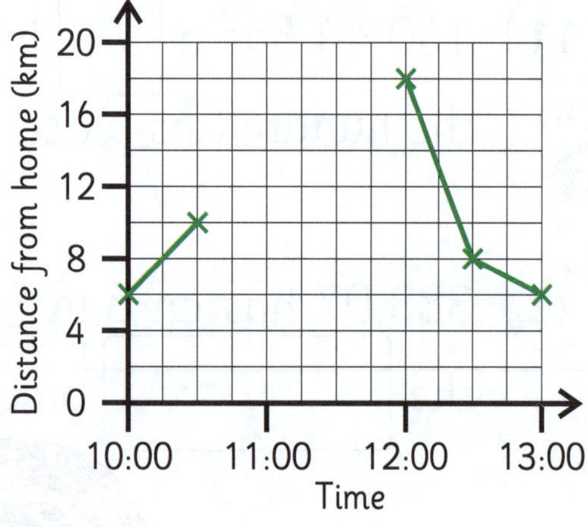

3 Adam was 9 km away from home at 18:30 and he returned home at 19:30.

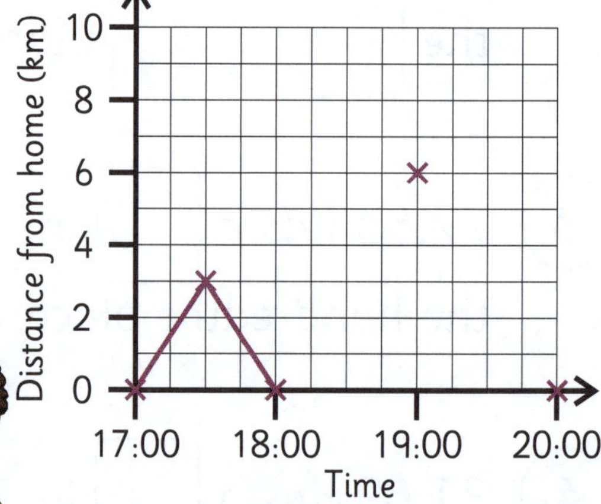

4 Adam was 10 km away from home between 15:00 and 15:30 and returned home at 17:00.

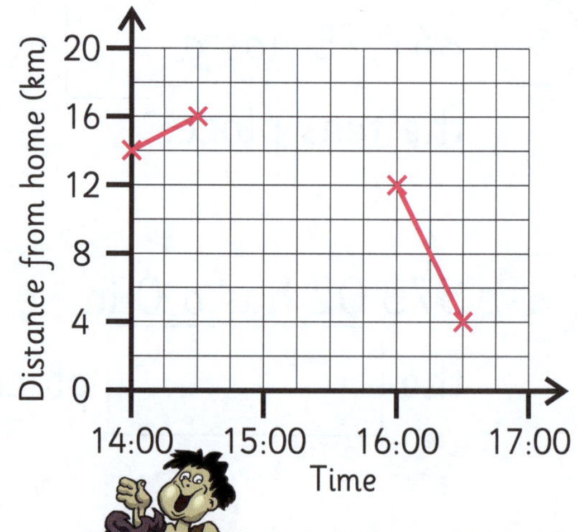

Today I scored ☐ out of 4.

Week 9 — Day 3

Look at the calculations in the box. Circle the one that is incorrect.

$8 \div 100 = 0.8$ *(circled)*

$2 \div 10 = 0.2$

$13 \div 10 = 1.3$

1
$5 \div 10 = 0.5$
$59 \div 10 = 0.59$
$65 \div 100 = 0.65$

6
$95 \div 10 = 0.95$
$1 \div 100 = 0.01$
$51 \div 100 = 0.51$

2
$9 \div 10 = 0.9$
$26 \div 100 = 0.26$
$82 \div 100 = 8.2$

7
$72 \div 10 = 7.2$
$8 \div 100 = 0.08$
$16 \div 100 = 0.016$

3
$83 \div 100 = 0.83$
$35 \div 10 = 3.5$
$6 \div 100 = 0.006$

8
$74 \div 100 = 0.74$
$80 \div 100 = 0.8$
$9 \div 10 = 0.09$

4
$2 \div 10 = 0.02$
$8 \div 100 = 0.08$
$55 \div 10 = 5.5$

9
$51 \div 10 = 5.1$
$12 \div 100 = 1.2$
$37 \div 100 = 0.37$

5
$5 \div 100 = 0.05$
$97 \div 10 = 0.97$
$4 \div 10 = 0.4$

10
$93 \div 10 = 9.3$
$36 \div 100 = 0.36$
$60 \div 10 = 0.6$

Today I scored ☐ out of 10.

Year 4 Maths — Summer Term

Week 9 — Day 4

The line graph shows how two plants grew over time. Use the graph to answer the question.

How much taller was plant A than plant B on Day 10?

15 mm

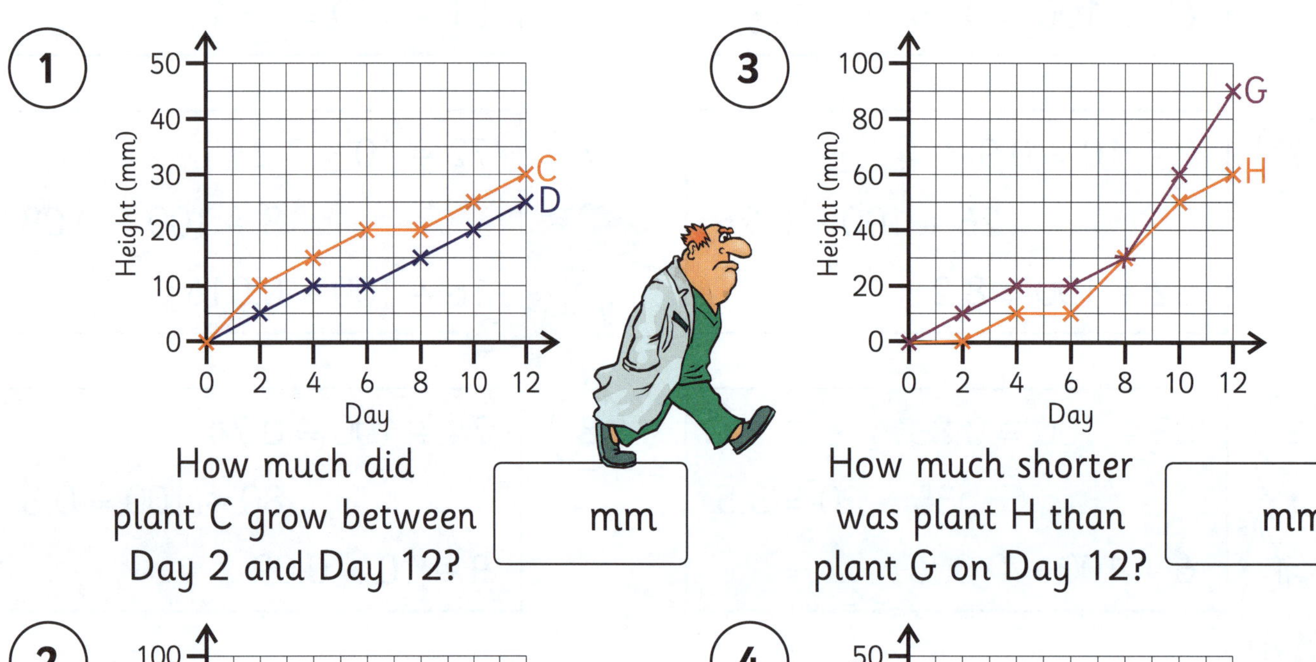

1 How much did plant C grow between Day 2 and Day 12? mm

3 How much shorter was plant H than plant G on Day 12? mm

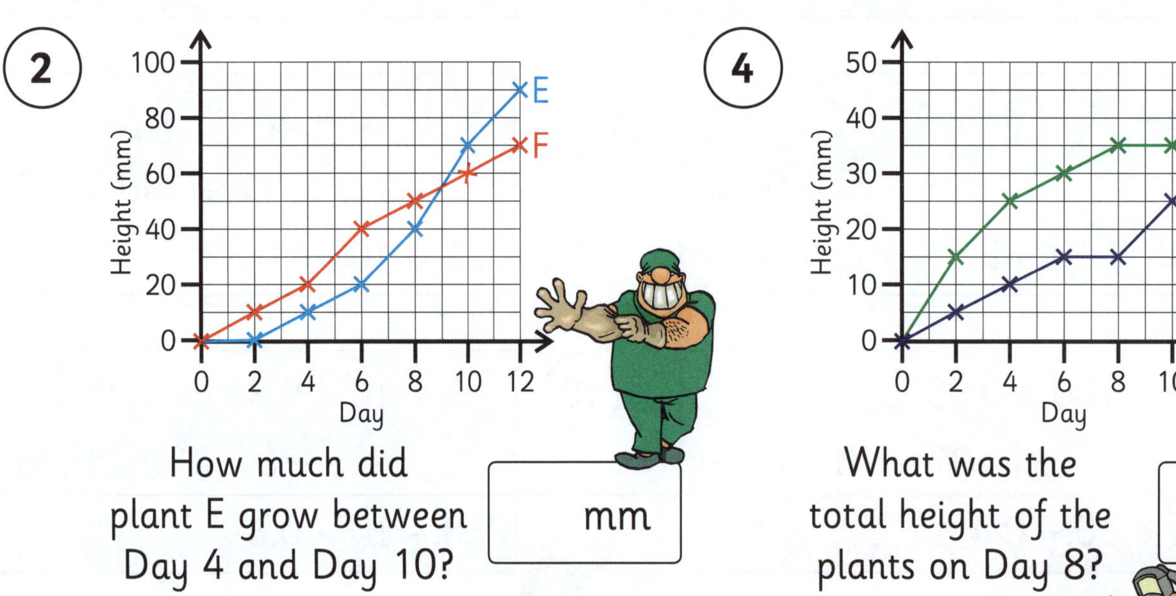

2 How much did plant E grow between Day 4 and Day 10? mm

4 What was the total height of the plants on Day 8? mm

Today I scored ☐ out of 4.

Week 9 — Day 5

Write the name of the person who has more money.

Ciaran has forty 1p coins and three 20p coins. Sidney has two 20p coins and ten more 1p coins than Ciaran.

1 Emma has fifty 1p coins and four 10p coins. Anjali has ten fewer 1p coins than Emma and has six 10p coins.

2 Ravi has thirty 2p coins and ten 20p coins. Bill has fifty more 2p coins and three fewer 20p coins than Ravi.

3 Alex has twenty 2p coins and six 50p coins. Kim has twice as many 2p coins and half as many 50p coins as Alex.

4 Jane has twenty 5p coins and twenty 10p coins. Aine has thirty more 5p coins than Jane and half as many 10p coins.

5 Nicki has one hundred 2p coins and ten 50p coins. Ellie has twice as many 2p coins and half as many 50p coins as Nicki.

6 Max has sixty 5p coins and twelve 50p coins. Sam has twenty more 5p coins and half as many 50p coins as Max.

7 Chanon has one hundred 5p coins and ten 20p coins. Rory has fifty more 5p coins than Chanon and has no 20p coins.

8 Victoria has seventy 2p coins and fifty 5p coins. Maria has twenty more 2p coins than Victoria and half as many 5p coins.

Today I scored [ ] out of 8.

Week 10 — Day 1

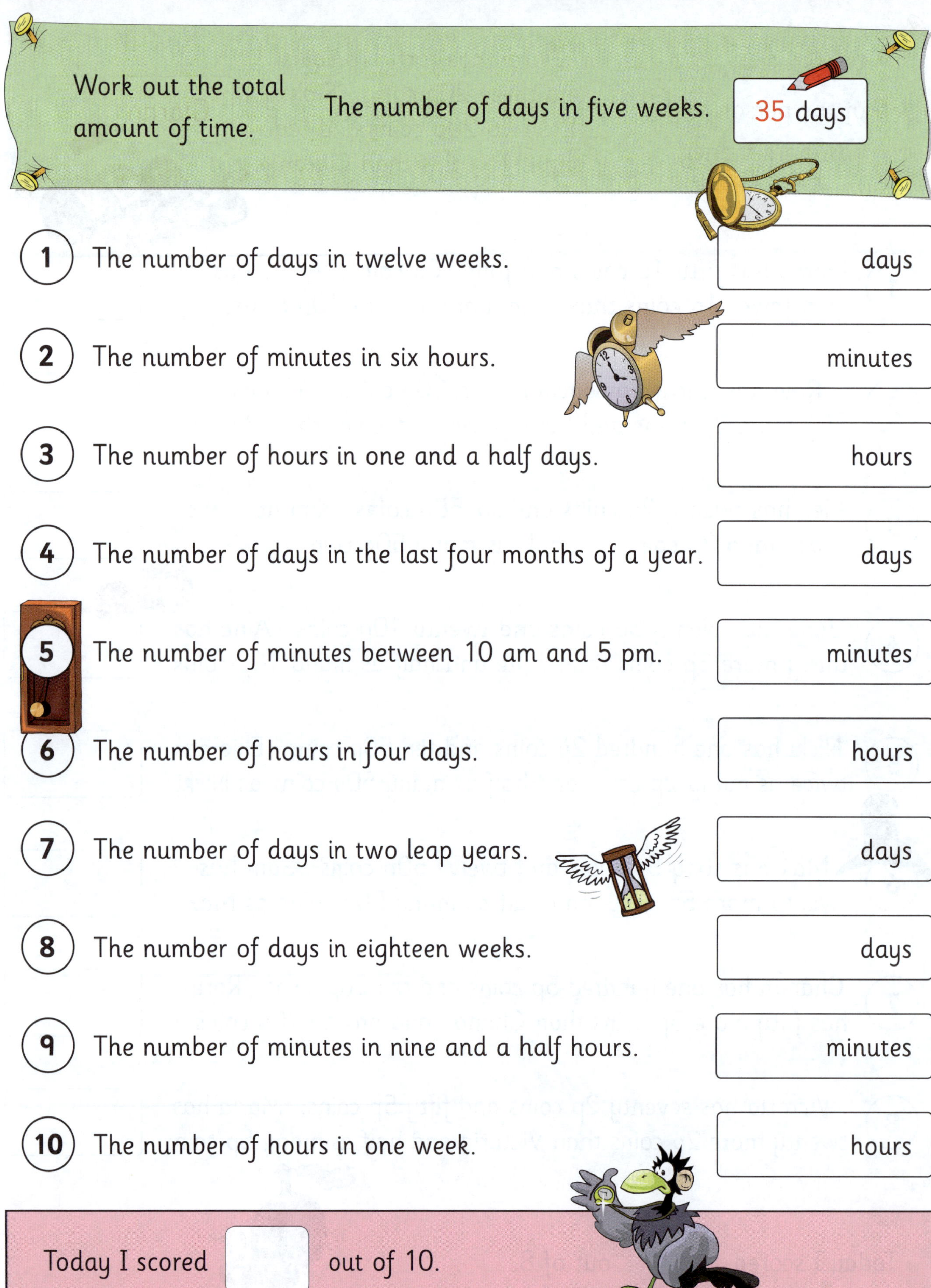

Work out the total amount of time.

The number of days in five weeks.　**35** days

1. The number of days in twelve weeks.　days
2. The number of minutes in six hours.　minutes
3. The number of hours in one and a half days.　hours
4. The number of days in the last four months of a year.　days
5. The number of minutes between 10 am and 5 pm.　minutes
6. The number of hours in four days.　hours
7. The number of days in two leap years.　days
8. The number of days in eighteen weeks.　days
9. The number of minutes in nine and a half hours.　minutes
10. The number of hours in one week.　hours

Today I scored ____ out of 10.

Week 10 — Day 2

Work out the answer
to the calculation.

```
  7 2 3 6
+ 1 6 3 7
─────────
  8 8 7 3
        1
```

1
```
  4 7 8 3
+ 5 1 3 5
─────────
```

6
```
  6 5 2 7
+ 2 6 1 5
─────────
```

2
```
  6 8 7 3
− 2 4 1 9
─────────
```

7
```
  9 5 3 2
− 8 7 1 5
─────────
```

3
```
  3 1 0 4
+ 1 5 9 6
─────────
```

8
```
  2 9 7 8
+ 5 6 8 4
─────────
```

4
```
  3 9 2 7
− 1 5 4 6
─────────
```

9
```
  5 8 7 1
− 3 9 7 8
─────────
```

5
```
  7 8 9 6
+ 2 0 9 9
─────────
```

10
```
  7 1 0 5
− 4 7 2 9
─────────
```

Today I scored ☐ out of 10.

Year 4 Maths — Summer Term

Week 10 — Day 3

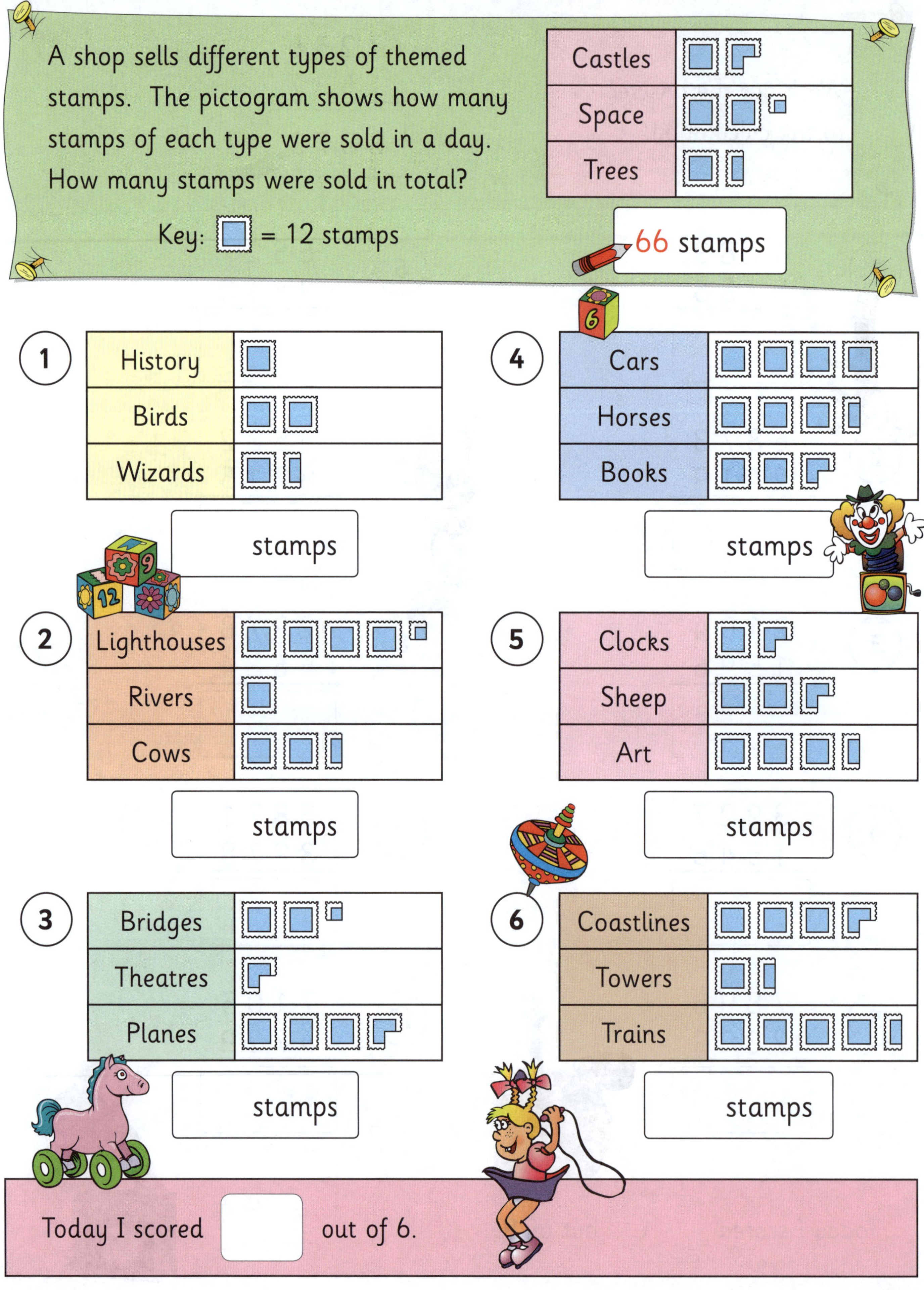

A shop sells different types of themed stamps. The pictogram shows how many stamps of each type were sold in a day. How many stamps were sold in total?

Key: ▢ = 12 stamps

Castles	
Space	
Trees	

66 stamps

1

History	
Birds	
Wizards	

_____ stamps

2

Lighthouses	
Rivers	
Cows	

_____ stamps

3

Bridges	
Theatres	
Planes	

_____ stamps

4

Cars	
Horses	
Books	

_____ stamps

5

Clocks	
Sheep	
Art	

_____ stamps

6

Coastlines	
Towers	
Trains	

_____ stamps

Today I scored [ ] out of 6.

Week 10 — Day 4

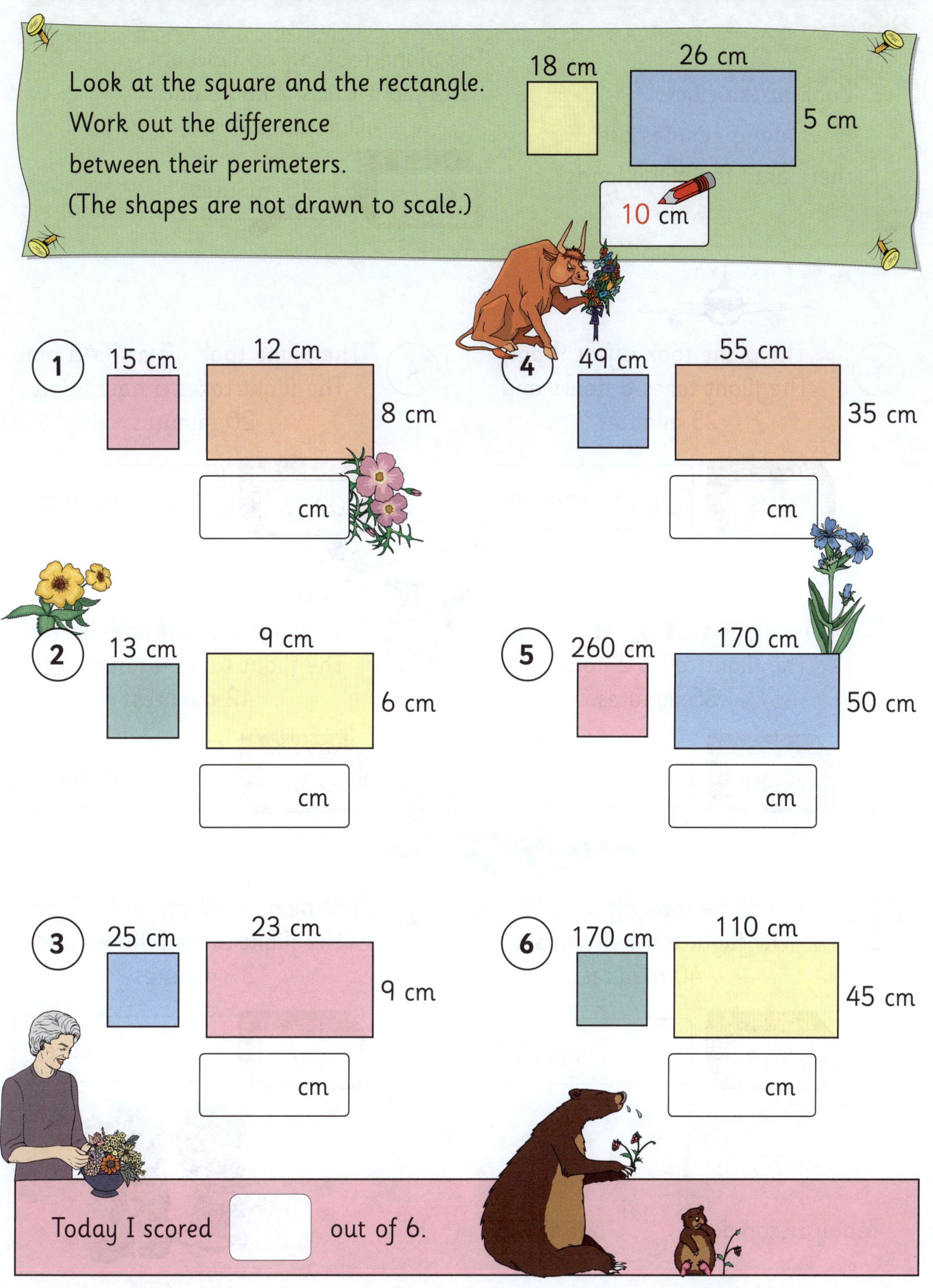

Look at the square and the rectangle.
Work out the difference
between their perimeters.
(The shapes are not drawn to scale.)

Today I scored [ ] out of 6.

Year 4 Maths — Summer Term

Week 10 — Day 5

Look at the clock.
How many minutes are
there until the plane lands?

The plane took off at 1:30 pm.
The flight takes 2 hours and
40 minutes.

15:40   30 minutes

1 The plane took off at 9 am.
The flight takes 8 hours and
25 minutes.

16:25   _______ minutes

4 The plane took off at 9:45 pm.
The flight takes 5 hours and
20 minutes.

02:15   _______ minutes

2 The plane took off at 1:30 pm.
The flight takes 2 hours and
35 minutes.

15:40   _______ minutes

5 The plane took off at 6:23 pm.
The flight takes 4 hours and
42 minutes.

22:50   _______ minutes

3 The plane took off at 4:15 pm.
The flight takes 3 hours and
40 minutes.

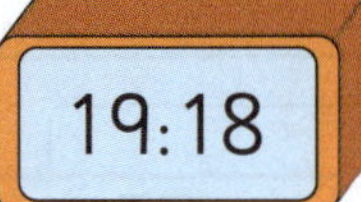

19:18   _______ minutes

6 The plane took off at 7:55 pm.
The flight takes 2 hours and
37 minutes.

21:22   _______ minutes

Today I scored [   ] out of 6.

Week 11 — Day 1

1. XXIII – XI =

2. LXXIII + IX =

3. XXXIX – XVIII =

4. LXXXIV + VIII =

5. LIII + XIX =

6. LXIV – XXV =

7. XLII + XV =

8. LXVII – XXXI =

9. XCV – LXXIX =

10. LIV + XXXVI =

11. XCVII – LVIII =

12. LXXXVI + LXXV =

Today I scored [ ] out of 12.

Week 11 — Day 2

The coordinates give the remaining vertices of a shape with one line of symmetry.

Plot the points and complete the shape.

Draw the line of symmetry on the shape.

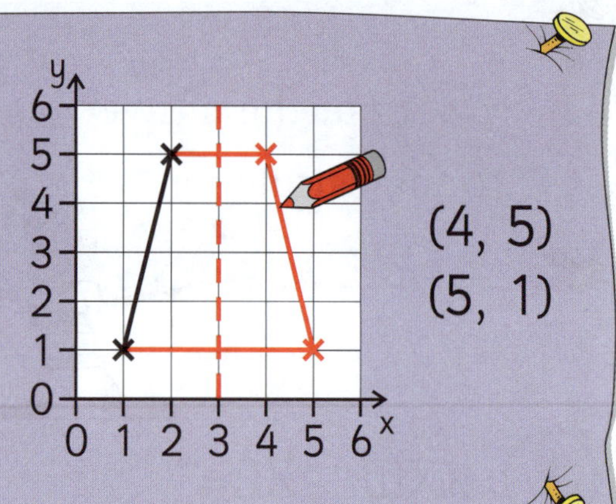

(4, 5)
(5, 1)

1

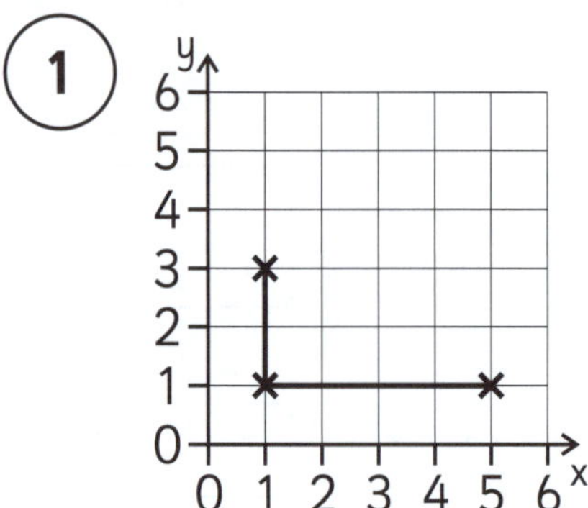

(5, 3)
(3, 5)

2

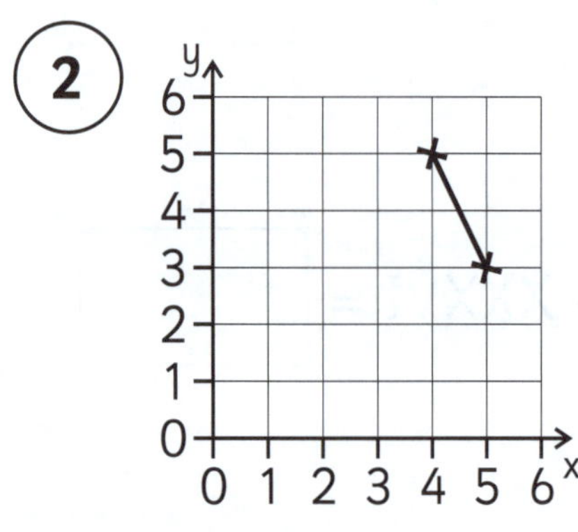

(4, 1)
(1, 3)

3

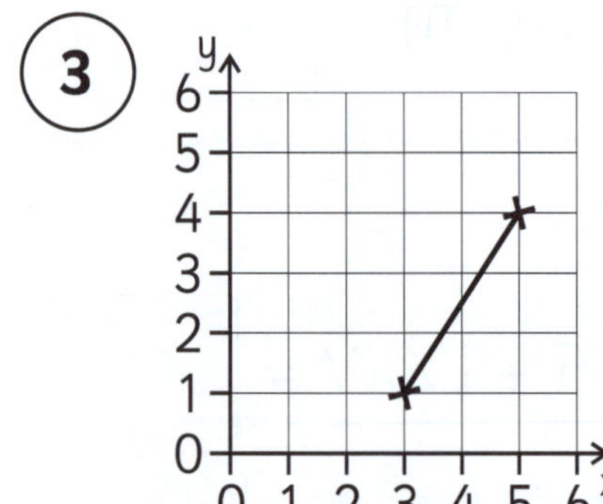

(1, 4)
(2, 5)
(4, 5)

4

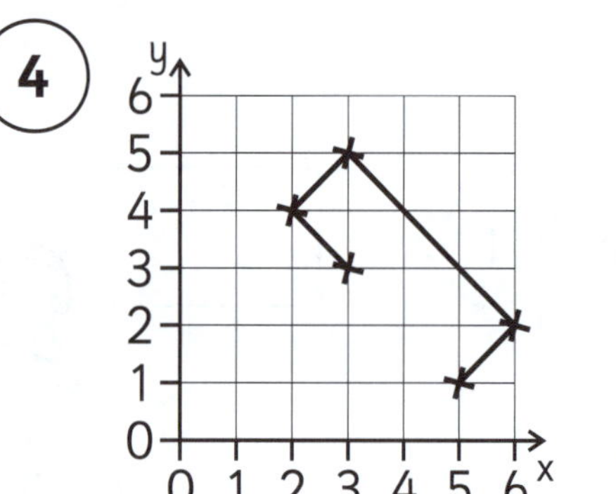

(2, 2)
(3, 1)
(4, 2)

5

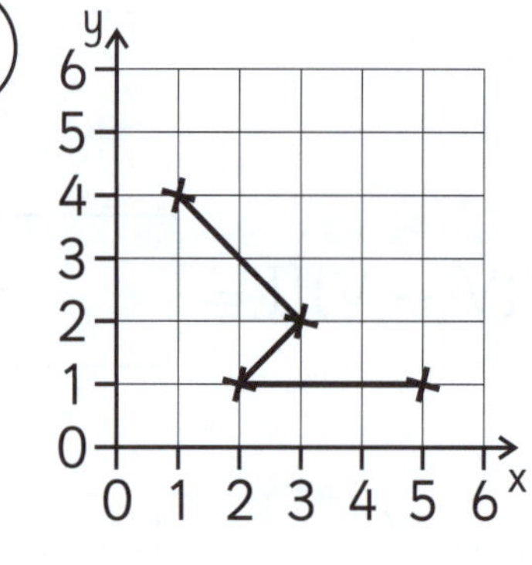

(2, 5)
(4, 3)
(5, 4)

6

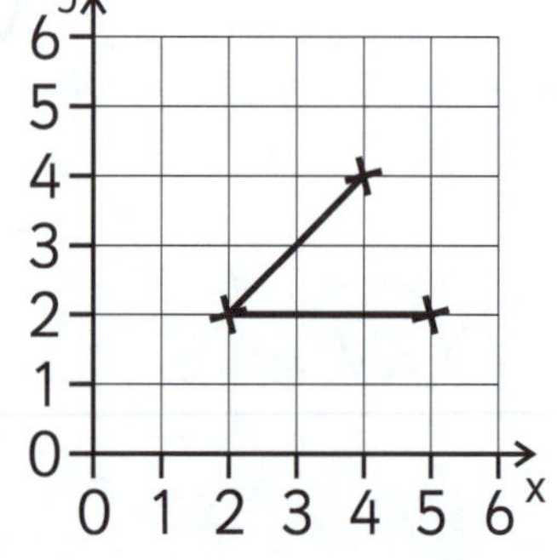

(6, 4)
(5, 6)
(2, 6)

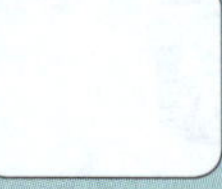

Today I scored [ ] out of 6.

Week 11 — Day 3

Fill in the box using <, > or =.

$2 \times 4 \times 11$ ⬚< $2 \times 5 \times 9$

1 $2 \times 6 \times 3$ ⬚ $3 \times 4 \times 3$

2 $2 \times 11 \times 2$ ⬚ $2 \times 5 \times 4$

3 $6 \times 2 \times 4$ ⬚ $8 \times 3 \times 2$

4 $3 \times 6 \times 3$ ⬚ $11 \times 4 \times 2$

5 $3 \times 7 \times 3$ ⬚ $5 \times 4 \times 2$

6 $3 \times 4 \times 6$ ⬚ $2 \times 9 \times 4$

7 $7 \times 2 \times 4$ ⬚ $3 \times 3 \times 9$

8 $6 \times 2 \times 9$ ⬚ $5 \times 11 \times 2$

9 $4 \times 8 \times 3$ ⬚ $5 \times 6 \times 2$

10 $4 \times 4 \times 5$ ⬚ $6 \times 6 \times 2$

11 $3 \times 9 \times 2$ ⬚ $4 \times 7 \times 3$

12 $6 \times 5 \times 5$ ⬚ $12 \times 4 \times 3$

Today I scored ⬚ out of 12.

  Year 4 Maths — Summer Term

Week 11 — Day 4

The table shows the results of a survey about people's favourite types of juice. Work out the total number of people who liked the two most popular types of juice. Write down the answer rounded to the nearest 10.

Juice	People
Orange	47
Pineapple	68
Tomato	98
Grapefruit	54

1

Juice	People
Pineapple	51
Apple	82
Papaya	48
Peach	46

4

Juice	People
Guava	61
Tomato	78
Peach	59
Strawberry	87

2

Juice	People
Grape	81
Apple	65
Cranberry	74
Melon	43

5

Juice	People
Orange	58
Grape	69
Pineapple	41
Papaya	77

3

Juice	People
Tropical	44
Guava	56
Strawberry	64
Orange	72

6

Juice	People
Tropical	86
Cranberry	79
Grapefruit	88
Melon	96

Today I scored [ ] out of 6.

Week 11 — Day 5

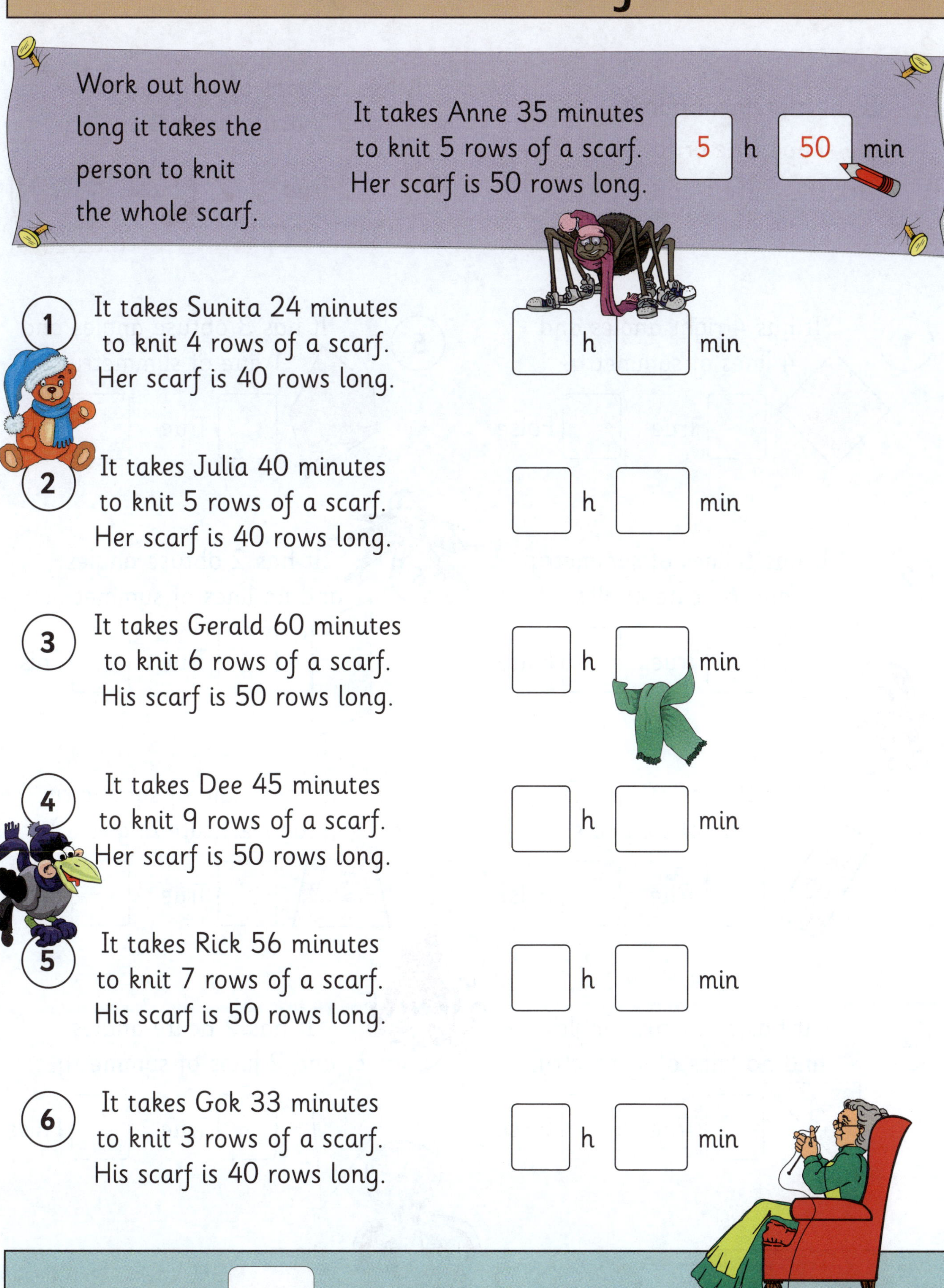

Work out how long it takes the person to knit the whole scarf.

It takes Anne 35 minutes to knit 5 rows of a scarf. Her scarf is 50 rows long.

1. It takes Sunita 24 minutes to knit 4 rows of a scarf. Her scarf is 40 rows long.

  h   min

2. It takes Julia 40 minutes to knit 5 rows of a scarf. Her scarf is 40 rows long.

  h   min

3. It takes Gerald 60 minutes to knit 6 rows of a scarf. His scarf is 50 rows long.

  h   min

4. It takes Dee 45 minutes to knit 9 rows of a scarf. Her scarf is 50 rows long.

  h   min

5. It takes Rick 56 minutes to knit 7 rows of a scarf. His scarf is 50 rows long.

  h   min

6. It takes Gok 33 minutes to knit 3 rows of a scarf. His scarf is 40 rows long.

  h   min

Today I scored   out of 6.

      Year 4 Maths — Summer Term

Week 12 — Day 1

Is the statement about the shape true or false? Tick the correct box.

It has no lines of symmetry and 2 acute angles.

[ ] True   [✓] False

1 It has 4 right angles and 4 lines of symmetry.

[ ] True   [ ] False

2 It has 6 lines of symmetry and 6 acute angles.

[ ] True   [ ] False

3 It has 2 lines of symmetry and no obtuse angles.

[ ] True   [ ] False

4 It has two acute angles and no lines of symmetry.

[ ] True   [ ] False

5 It has 3 obtuse angles and 1 line of symmetry.

[ ] True   [ ] False

6 It has 2 obtuse angles and no lines of symmetry.

[ ] True   [ ] False

7 It has 1 line of symmetry and 2 acute angles.

[ ] True   [ ] False

8 It has 2 acute angles and 2 lines of symmetry.

[ ] True   [ ] False

Today I scored [ ] out of 8.

Week 12 — Day 2

Round the amount to the nearest unit given.

What is 8.3 kg to the nearest kilogram?

1. What is 2.8 g to the nearest gram? ___ g

2. What is 55.2 ml to the nearest millilitre? ___ ml

3. What is 45.6 kg to the nearest kilogram? ___ kg

4. What is 11.5 m to the nearest metre? ___ m

5. What is 41 mm to the nearest centimetre? ___ cm

6. What is 91.4 km to the nearest kilometre? ___ km

7. What is 424.5 kg to the nearest kilogram? ___ kg

8. What is 2100 m to the nearest kilometre? ___ km

9. What is 5600 ml to the nearest litre? ___ l

10. What is 6500 m to the nearest kilometre? ___ km

Today I scored [ ] out of 10.

Year 4 Maths — Summer Term

Week 12 — Day 3

How far did the person travel in total?

Dev ran 4.5 km and swam 680 m.

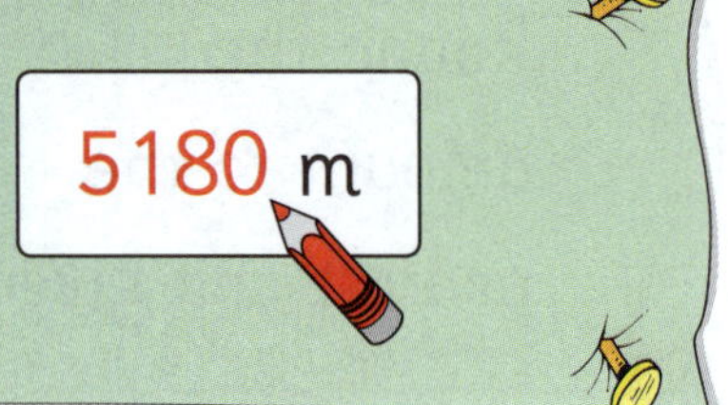

1 Jonny ran 7 km and swam 900 m.

[ ] m

2 Nicole swam 855 m and ran 8.1 km.

[ ] m

3 Zoe swam 650 m and cycled 8.6 km.

[ ] m

4 Elodie swam 550 m and ran 6.8 km.

[ ] m

5 Mark ran 2.8 km and swam 295 m.

[ ] m

6 Zain cycled 6.2 km and swam 930 m.

[ ] m

7 Alastair cycled 5.7 km and swam 875 m.

[ ] m

8 Aisha swam 735 m and cycled 2.6 km.

[ ] m

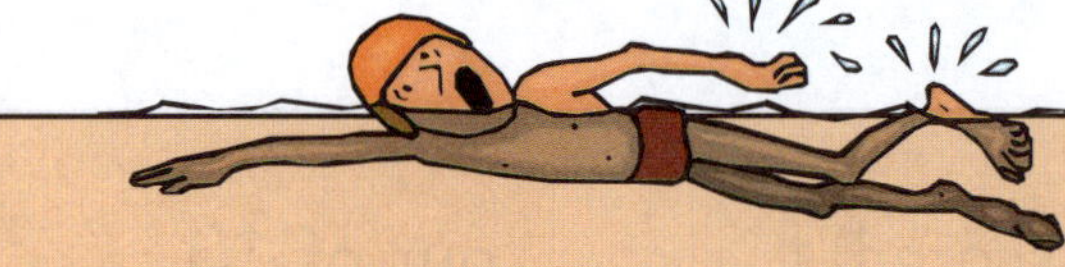

Today I scored [ ] out of 8.

Week 12 — Day 4

Use the number fact to help you answer the calculation.

$34 \times 11 = 374$

$37 \times 11 = $ 407 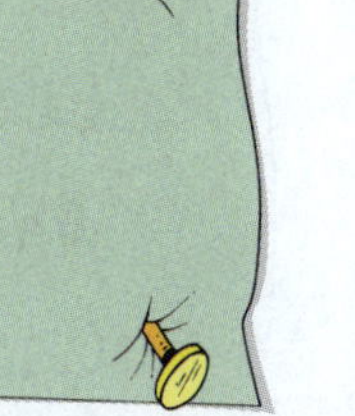

1 $47 \times 5 = 235$

$57 \times 5 = $

2 $77 \times 8 = 616$

$79 \times 8 = $

3 $65 \times 9 = 585$

$69 \times 9 = $

4 $32 \times 11 = 352$

$32 \times 12 = $

5 $89 \times 7 = 623$

$87 \times 7 = $

6 $26 \times 12 = 312$

$26 \times 11 = $

7 $145 \times 6 = 870$

$154 \times 6 = $

8 $41 \times 12 = 492$

$34 \times 12 = $

9 $44 \times 11 = 484$

$52 \times 11 = $

10 $107 \times 7 = 749$

$115 \times 7 = $

11 $92 \times 9 = 828$

$85 \times 9 = $

12 $63 \times 12 = 756$

$54 \times 12 = $

Today I scored [ ] out of 12.

Year 4 Maths — Summer Term

Week 12 — Day 5

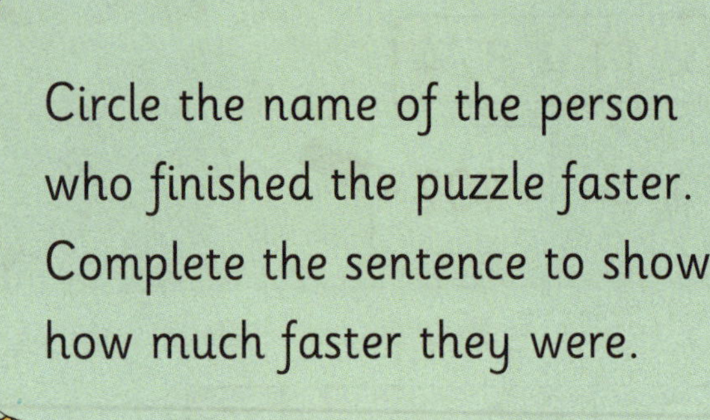

Circle the name of the person who finished the puzzle faster. Complete the sentence to show how much faster they were.

Kate completed a puzzle in $4\frac{1}{2}$ minutes. Lisa took 225 seconds.

Kate / (Lisa) completed the puzzle faster, by **45** seconds.

1) James completed a puzzle in $6\frac{1}{2}$ minutes. Steve took 300 seconds.

James / Steve completed the puzzle faster, by ____ seconds.

2) Lucy completed a puzzle in 500 seconds. Lakisha took $8\frac{1}{2}$ minutes.

Lucy / Lakisha completed the puzzle faster, by ____ seconds.

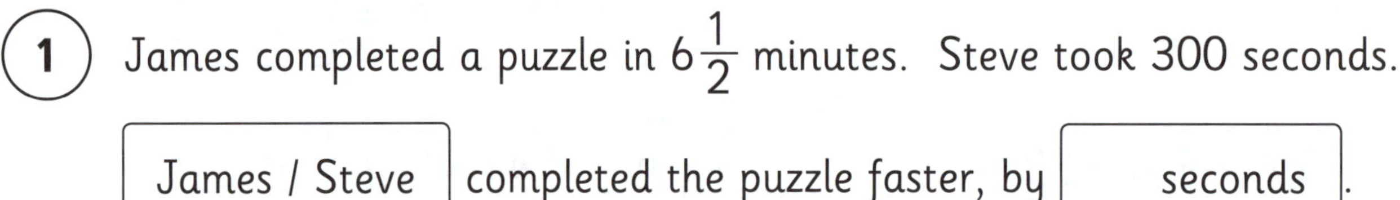

3) Jamal completed a puzzle in 140 minutes. Keith took $2\frac{1}{4}$ hours.

Jamal / Keith completed the puzzle faster, by ____ minutes.

4) Nick completed a puzzle in 730 seconds. Dan took $11\frac{1}{2}$ minutes.

Nick / Dan completed the puzzle faster, by ____ seconds.

5) Cath completed a puzzle in 260 minutes. Sophie took $4\frac{3}{4}$ hours.

Cath / Sophie completed the puzzle faster, by ____ minutes.

Today I scored ____ out of 5.

Answers

Week 1 — Day 1

1. 300, 400, 500, **600, 700, 800**
2. 600, 650, 700, **750, 800, 850**
3. 1000, 2000, 3000, **4000, 5000, 6000**
4. 350, 375, 400, **425, 450, 475**
5. 6600, 7600, 8600, **9600, 10600, 11600**
6. 875, 900, 925, **950, 975, 1000**
7. 7015, 6015, 5015, **4015, 3015, 2015**
8. 1250, 1225, 1200, **1175, 1150, 1125**

Week 1 — Day 2

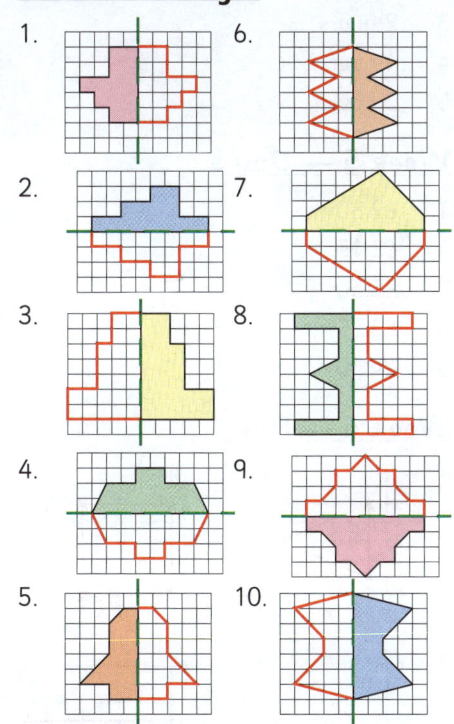

Week 1 — Day 3

1. 6.4 km
2. 9500 g
3. 10 km
4. 5000 ml
5. 1900 cm
6. 70 m
7. 2 minutes
8. 400 kg
9. 38.5 litres
10. 450 minutes
11. 24 m
12. 600 seconds

Week 1 — Day 4

1. 350
2. 625
3. 375
4. 775
5. 1650
6. 6750
7. 75
8. 425
9. 5575
10. 2475

Week 1 — Day 5

1. 4000 m
2. 150 km
3. 7000 m
4. 200 km
5. 12 000 m
6. 275 km
7. 18 000 m

Week 2 — Day 1

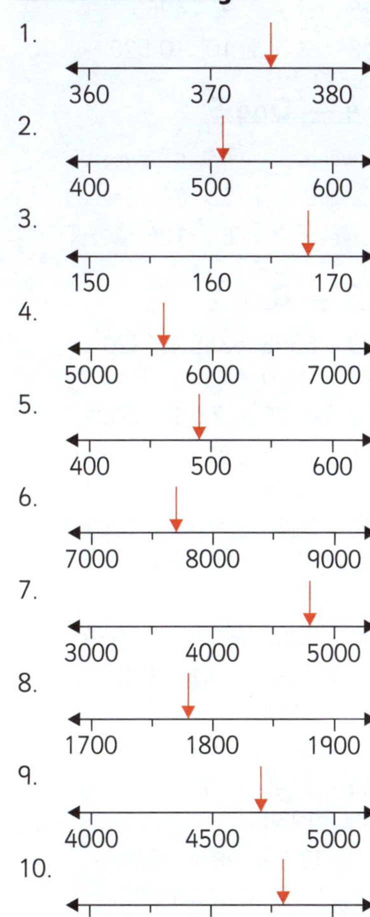

1. (360, 370, 380)
2. (400, 500, 600)
3. (150, 160, 170)
4. (5000, 6000, 7000)
5. (400, 500, 600)
6. (7000, 8000, 9000)
7. (3000, 4000, 5000)
8. (1700, 1800, 1900)
9. (4000, 4500, 5000)
10. (750, 850, 950)

Week 2 — Day 2

1. 52 > 48
2. 50 > 48
3. 54 < 56
4. 67 < 80
5. 49 < 50
6. 72 > 70
7. 6 = 6
8. 50 > 49
9. 108 > 106
10. 132 = 132

Week 2 — Day 3

1. 552
2. 820
3. 1236
4. 4884
5. 2610
6. 2416
7. 6520
8. 3834
9. 4151
10. 4466

Week 2 — Day 4

1. 37
2. 64
3. 96
4. 149
5. 95
6. 115
7. 116
8. 115
9. 180
10. 156

Week 2 — Day 5

1. Yes (He needs £138.)
2. Yes (She needs £201.)
3. No (She needs £243.)
4. No (She needs £177.)
5. Yes (He needs £207.)
6. No (He needs £156.)
7. No (She needs £342.)

Week 3 — Day 1

1. E.g. 97 − 8 + 5 or 97 + 5 − 8 = **94**
2. E.g. 50 + 19 − 17 or 50 − 17 + 19 = **52**
3. E.g. 45 + 31 − 13 or 45 − 13 + 31 = **63**
4. E.g. 14 + 79 − 22 or 14 − 22 + 79 = **71**
5. E.g. 72 − 38 + 57 or 72 + 57 − 38 = **91**
6. E.g. 66 + 55 − 34 or 66 − 34 + 55 = **87**

Week 3 — Day 2

1. 3 — 5, 15 — 1
2. 1 — 21, 7 — 3
3. 2 — 6, 12 — 1, 3 — 4
4. 6 — 3, 9 — 2, 1 — 18
5. 4 — 9, 3 — 12, 1 — 36
6. 8 — 6, 2 — 24, 4 — 12, 48 — 1
7. 25 — 4, 20 — 5, 50 — 2
8. 10 — 6, 3 — 20, 12 — 5, 2 — 30

Week 3 — Day 3

1. 130 g
2. 60 g
3. 100 g
4. 10 g
5. 150 g
6. 80 g

Week 3 — Day 4

1. 1232
2. 3090
3. 6033
4. 5691
5. 1984
6. 3999

Week 3 — Day 5

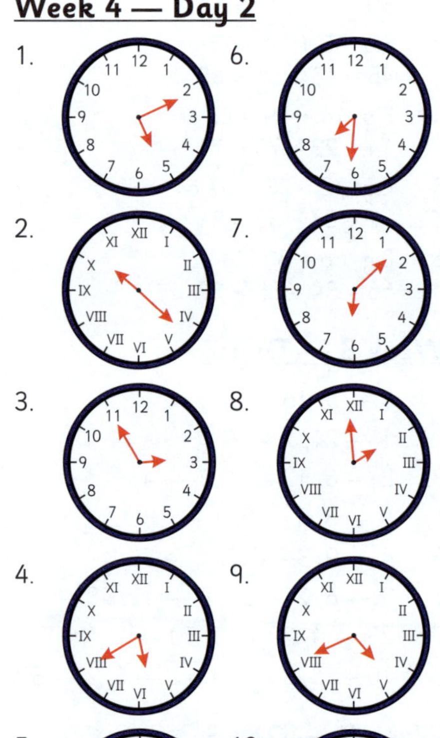

1. $\frac{4}{8}$ ×6 → $\frac{24}{48}$ ×6

2. $\frac{3}{5}$ ×4 → $\frac{12}{20}$ ×4

3. $\frac{32}{40}$ ÷8 → $\frac{4}{5}$ ÷8

4. $\frac{1}{7}$ ×3 → $\frac{3}{21}$ ×3

5. $\frac{2}{5}$ ×11 → $\frac{22}{55}$ ×11

6. $\frac{72}{96}$ ÷12 → $\frac{6}{8}$ ÷12

7. $\frac{28}{56}$ ÷7 → $\frac{4}{8}$ ÷7

8. $\frac{72}{108}$ ÷9 → $\frac{8}{12}$ ÷9

Week 4 — Day 1

1. **0.8**, 0.9, 1.0, 1.1, **1.2**, **1.3**
2. 0.13, 0.14, **0.15**, **0.16**, 0.17, **0.18**
3. 0.04, 0.06, 0.08, **0.10**, **0.12**, **0.14**
4. 0.45, 0.50, 0.55, **0.60**, **0.65**, **0.70**
5. **1.30**, 1.31, **1.32**, 1.33, **1.34**, 1.35
6. **0.05**, **0.10**, 0.15, 0.20, 0.25, **0.30**
7. **0.64**, 0.66, 0.68, **0.70**, **0.72**, 0.74
8. **0.98**, **0.99**, **1.00**, 1.01, 1.02, 1.03

Week 4 — Day 2

1. 6.
2. 7.
3. 8.
4. 9.
5. 10.

Week 4 — Day 3

1. $\frac{1}{2}$
2. $\frac{5}{20}$
3. $\frac{2}{3}$
4. $\frac{6}{16}$
5. $\frac{4}{10}$
6. $\frac{1}{4}$
7. $\frac{4}{5}$
8. $\frac{3}{10}$
9. $\frac{1}{5}$
10. $\frac{7}{10}$

Week 4 — Day 4

1. 2868
2. 6358
3. 1841
4. 8525
5. 2948
6. 1986
7. 6202
8. 2963
9. 4955
10. 10 520

Week 4 — Day 5

1. 20 sweets
2. 44 sweets
3. 50 sweets
4. 47 sweets
5. 64 sweets
6. 126 sweets

Week 5 — Day 1

1. 1920 + 6358, 6358 + 1920 or 8278 − 1920
2. 7812 − 4775 or 7812 − 3037
3. 4324 + 2827, 2827 + 4324 or 7151 − 4324
4. 9247 − 7946 or 9247 − 1301
5. 40.4 + 20.4, 20.4 + 40.4 or 60.8 − 40.4
6. 9221 − 5282 or 9221 − 3939
7. 4154 + 1667, 1667 + 4154 or 5821 − 4154
8. 56.9 − 30.5 or 56.9 − 26.4
9. 1954 + 4495, 4495 + 1954 or 6449 − 1954
10. 98.1 − 17.5 or 98.1 − 80.6
11. 19.8 + 57.8, 57.8 + 19.8 or 77.6 − 19.8
12. 8643 − 1724 or 8643 − 6919

Week 5 — Day 2

1. To the nearest 100 = **4100**
   To the nearest 1000 = **4000**
2. To the nearest 100 = **3500**
   To the nearest 1000 = **4000**
3. To the nearest 100 = **7200**
   To the nearest 1000 = **7000**
4. To the nearest 100 = **9200**
   To the nearest 1000 = **9000**
5. To the nearest 100 = **6700**
   To the nearest 1000 = **7000**
6. To the nearest 100 = **8800**
   To the nearest 1000 = **9000**
7. To the nearest 100 = **2300**
   To the nearest 1000 = **2000**
8. To the nearest 100 = **1800**
   To the nearest 1000 = **2000**
9. To the nearest 100 = **900**
   To the nearest 1000 = **1000**
10. To the nearest 100 = **7500**
    To the nearest 1000 = **7000**

Week 5 — Day 3

1. 42, 37, 35
2. 84, 78, 76
3. 66, 72
4. 16, 23, 19
5. 25, 34, 28
6. 51, 47, 54
7. 55, 64
8. 92, 89, 86
9. 7, 14
10. 97, 101, 98

Week 5 — Day 4

1. 10 days
2. 6 days
3. 2 hours
4. 4 hours
5. 2 hours

Week 5 — Day 5

1. £2.80
2. £3.15
3. £5.50
4. £3.55
5. £4.30

Week 6 — Day 1

1. 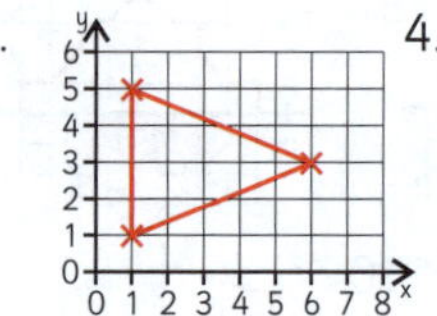
2. 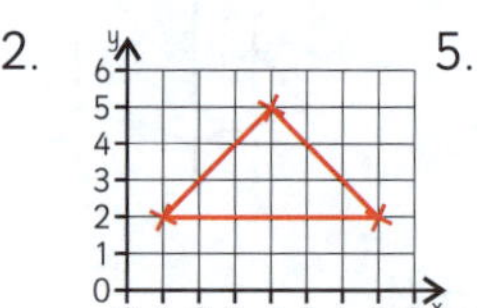
3. 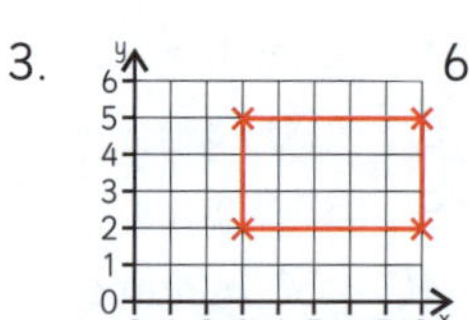
4. 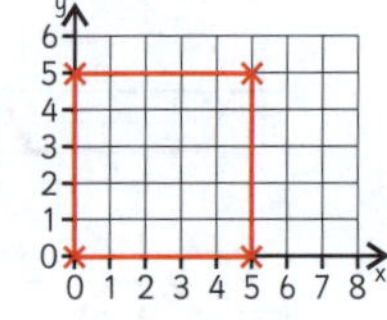
5. 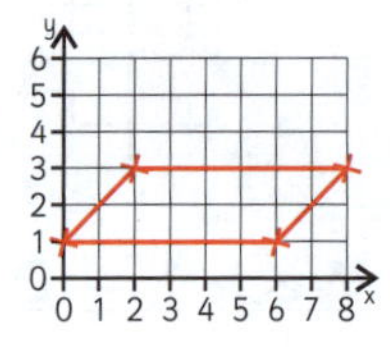
6. 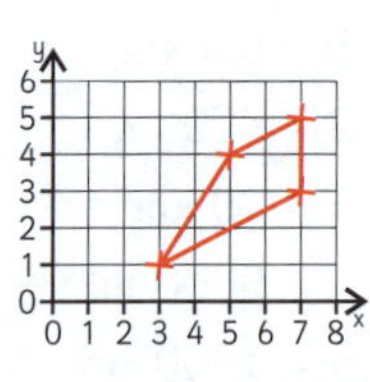

Week 6 — Day 2

1. 32
2. 45
3. 120
4. 60
5. 110
6. 108
7. 56
8. 84
9. 132
10. 360
11. 120
12. 150

Week 6 — Day 3

1. **3** squares **left** and **3** squares **down**.
2. **6** squares **left** and **4** squares **up**.
3. **4** squares **right** and **4** squares **up**.
4. **3** squares **right** and **3** squares **down**.
5. **5** squares **left** and **2** squares **up**.
6. **7** squares **left** and **2** squares **down**.

Week 6 — Day 4

1. $\frac{11}{25}$
2. $\frac{3}{17}$
3. $\frac{21}{58}$
4. $\frac{13}{45}$
5. $\frac{35}{64}$
6. $\frac{113}{181}$
7. $\frac{59}{128}$
8. $\frac{149}{205}$

Week 6 — Day 5

1. 260 cm
2. 129 mm
3. 6650 g
4. 8800 ml
5. 8650 g
6. 901 cm
7. 580 cm
8. 6402 m
9. 781 m
10. 2332 m

Week 7 — Day 1

1. 3.6, 4, **4.1**, **4.4** | 5.3, 5, **5.4**, **4.6**
2. **6.4**, 6, **6.3** | **7.2**, **6.5**, 7, **6.7**, **6.6**
3. **9.2**, 9, **8.7** | **9.8**, 10, **9.5**, **10.2**, **9.9**
4. **7.6**, **8.2**, 8, **8.4**, **8.1** | **8.5**, 9, **9.3**
5. **1.3**, 1, **1.4**, **0.8** | **1.9**, 2, **2.3**, **1.5**
6. **0.1**, 0, **0.2**, **0.4** | **1.2**, **0.5**, 1, **0.6**

Week 7 — Day 2

1. 852
2. 786
3. 3784
4. 204
5. 2376
6. 106
7. 6048
8. 116
9. 5383
10. 42

Week 7 — Day 3

1. $6.3 + 2 + 0.6 = 8.9$
2. $6.5 + 3 + 0.3 = 9.8$
3. $8.4 + 1 + 0.5 = 9.9$
4. $6.1 + 1 + 0.7 = 7.8$
5. $16.1 + 3 + 0.4 = 19.5$
6. $33.1 + 2 + 0.6 = 35.7$
7. $64 + 5 + 0.9 = 69.9$
8. $56.5 + 20 + 6 + 0.2 = 82.7$
9. $31.9 + 20 + 5 + 0.6 = 57.5$
10. $26.5 + 10 + 3 + 0.8 = 40.3$

Week 7 — Day 4

1. $0.1 + 0.6 = 0.7$
2. $0.5 + 0.1 = 0.6$
3. $0.25 + 0.01 = 0.26$
4. $0.5 + 0.4 = 0.9$
5. $0.02 + 0.75 = 0.77$
6. $0.04 + 0.09 = 0.13$
7. $0.3 + 0.65 = 0.95$
8. $0.8 + 0.5 = 1.3$
9. $0.3 + 0.54 = 0.84$
10. $0.75 + 0.43 = 1.18$

Week 7 — Day 5

1. 37 people
2. 108 people
3. 25 people
4. 101 people
5. 248 people
6. 387 people

Week 8 — Day 1

1. D = (1, 1), E = (2, 5), F = (5, 1)
2. G = (2, 3), H = (3, 1), I = (5, 4)
3. J = (0, 2), K = (3, 4), L = (5, 3)
4. M = (1, 6), N = (2, 0), O = (5, 5)
5. P = (0, 5), Q = (4, 0), R = (6, 2)
6. S = (0, 1), T = (3, 6), U = (5, 0)

Week 8 — Day 2

1. 24.56 m, 23.57 m, 23.66 m
2. 4.50 ml, 5.04 ml, 5.34 ml
3. 67.26 kg, 66.72 kg, 68.25 kg
4. 151.30 g, 115.47 g
5. 5.91 kg, 6.79 kg
6. 4.24 cm, 3.35 cm, 4.05 cm
7. 56.77 l, 55.89 l, 56.69 l
8. 16.17 g, 17.07 g, 16.99 g
9. 11.95 m, 10.99 m
10. 296.95 l, 296.76 l

Week 8 — Day 3

1. 50 m
2. 47 m
3. 54 m
4. 79 m
5. 81 m
6. 92 m
7. 115 m
8. 126 m

Week 8 — Day 4

1. 8 minutes
2. 23 minutes
3. 38 minutes
4. 183 minutes
5. 17 minutes

Week 8 — Day 5

1. 0.7 m
2. 30.7 cm
3. 11.2 cm
4. 0.31 m
5. 22.03 cm
6. 0.72 m
7. 321.39 mm
8. 0.69 m
9. 29.04 cm
10. 0.27 m
11. 467.62 mm
12. 40.89 cm

Week 9 — Day 1

1. 3
2. tens
3. 3
4. 6
5. 4
6. tenths
7. 2
8. hundredths
9. 7
10. hundreds
11. 4
12. tens

Week 9 — Day 2

1.

2.

3. 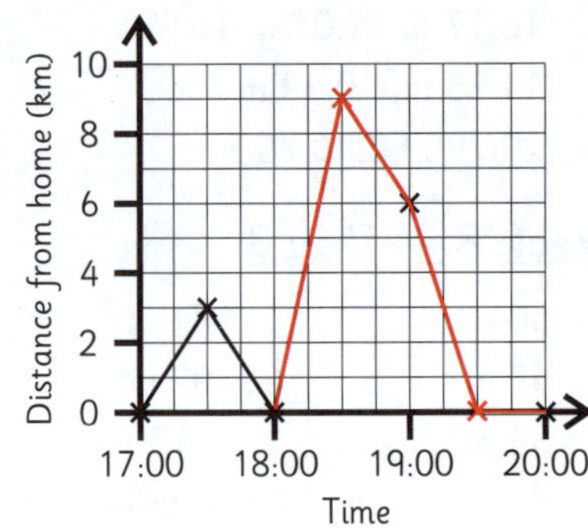

4. 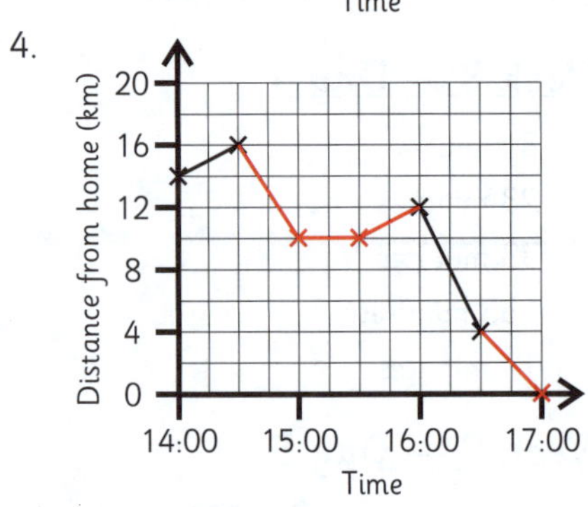

Week 9 — Day 3

1. $59 \div 10 = 0.59$
2. $82 \div 100 = 8.2$
3. $6 \div 100 = 0.006$
4. $2 \div 10 = 0.02$
5. $97 \div 10 = 0.97$
6. $95 \div 10 = 0.95$
7. $16 \div 100 = 0.016$
8. $9 \div 10 = 0.09$
9. $12 \div 100 = 1.2$
10. $60 \div 10 = 0.6$

Week 9 — Day 4

1. 20 mm
2. 60 mm
3. 30 mm
4. 50 mm

Week 9 — Day 5

1. Anjali
2. Bill
3. Alex
4. Aine
5. Nicki
6. Max
7. Rory
8. Victoria

Week 10 — Day 1

1. 84 days
2. 360 minutes
3. 36 hours
4. 122 days
5. 420 minutes
6. 96 hours
7. 732 days
8. 126 days
9. 570 minutes
10. 168 hours

Week 10 — Day 2

1. 9918
2. 4454
3. 4700
4. 2381
5. 9995
6. 9142
7. 817
8. 8662
9. 1893
10. 2376

Week 10 — Day 3

1. 54 stamps
2. 93 stamps
3. 81 stamps
4. 123 stamps
5. 96 stamps
6. 117 stamps

Week 10 — Day 4

1. $60 - 40 =$ **20** cm
2. $52 - 30 =$ **22** cm
3. $100 - 64 =$ **36** cm
4. $196 - 180 =$ **16** cm
5. $1040 - 440 =$ **600** cm
6. $680 - 310 =$ **370** cm

Week 10 — Day 5

1. 60 minutes
2. 25 minutes
3. 37 minutes
4. 50 minutes
5. 15 minutes
6. 70 minutes

Week 11 — Day 1

1. 12
2. 82
3. 21
4. 92
5. 72
6. 39
7. 57
8. 36
9. 16
10. 90
11. 39
12. 161

Week 11 — Day 2

1. 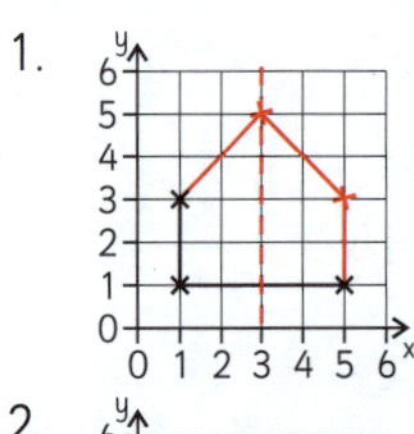
4. 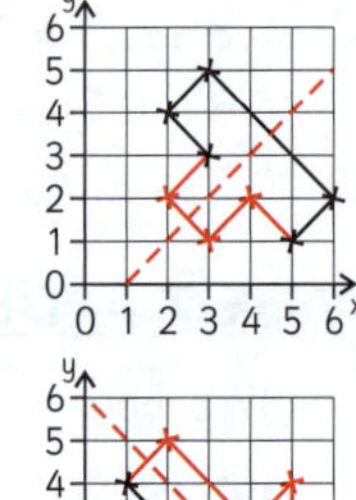
2. 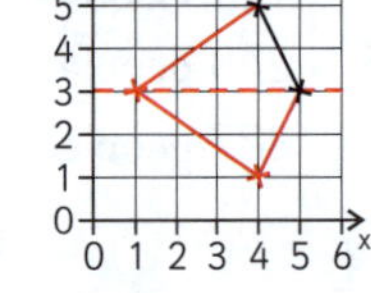
5. 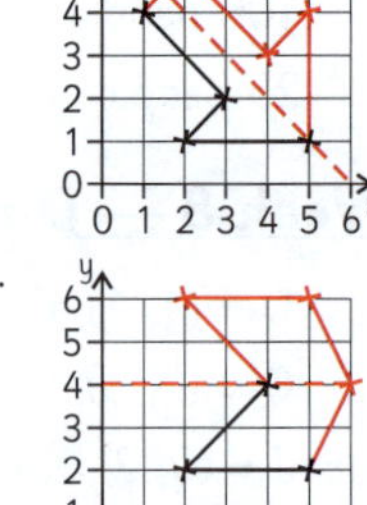
3. 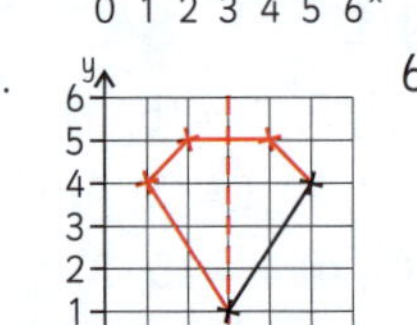

Week 11 — Day 3

1. $36 = 36$
2. $44 > 40$
3. $48 = 48$
4. $54 < 88$
5. $63 > 40$
6. $72 = 72$
7. $56 < 81$
8. $108 < 110$
9. $96 > 60$
10. $80 > 72$
11. $54 < 84$
12. $150 > 144$

Week 11 — Day 4

1. 130
2. 160
3. 140
4. 170
5. 150
6. 180

Week 11 — Day 5

1. 4 h 0 min
2. 5 h 20 min
3. 8 h 20 min
4. 4 h 10 min
5. 6 h 40 min
6. 7 h 20 min

Week 12 — Day 1

1. True
2. False
3. True
4. False
5. False
6. True
7. True
8. False

Week 12 — Day 2

1. 3 g
2. 55 ml
3. 46 kg
4. 12 m
5. 4 cm
6. 91 km
7. 425 kg
8. 2 km
9. 6 l
10. 7 km

Week 12 — Day 3

1. 7900 m
2. 8955 m
3. 9250 m
4. 7350 m
5. 3095 m
6. 7130 m
7. 6575 m
8. 3335 m

Week 12 — Day 4

1. 285
2. 632
3. 621
4. 384
5. 609
6. 286
7. 924
8. 408
9. 572
10. 805
11. 765
12. 648

Week 12 — Day 5

1. **Steve** completed the puzzle faster, by **90** seconds.
2. **Lucy** completed the puzzle faster, by **10** seconds.
3. **Keith** completed the puzzle faster, by **5** minutes.
4. **Dan** completed the puzzle faster, by **40** seconds.
5. **Cath** completed the puzzle faster, by **25** minutes.

Answers